TIES

TIES

Avril Hart

Costume & Fashion Press
an imprint of
Quite Specific Media Group Ltd.
New York

First published by V&A Publications, 1998

This edition published by:
Costume & Fashion Press, an imprint of
Quite Specific Media Group Ltd
260 Fifth Avenue, Suite 703
New York, NY 10001

(212)725-5377 voice, (212)725-8506 fax
email:info@quitespecificmedia.com

*Other Quite Specific Media Group Ltd
imprints:*
Drama Publishers
By Design Press
EntertainmentPro
Jade Rabbit

http://www.quitespecificmedia.com

ISBN 0-89676-229-7

Designed by Avril Broadley

Printed in Hong Kong

Jacket illustrations
Front: Pleated tie, shot silk
in blue and purple. Japanese,
1997. By Issey Miyake.
T.258–1997
Back: Mannequin of designer
ties in the V&A collection.
European, 1980s and
1990s. Styled by Sue Milner.
Mannequin courtesy of
Showbizz.

Title page: Printed silk
satin tie. British, 1960s.
By Frederick Theak.
T.209–1992

Frontispiece: Cartoon from
Punch, 1853. The style of
bow tie worn here by Frank
was also called a 'once
around tie'.
National Art Library (NAL); V&A

Contents

Acknowledgements

I have received much help and advice whilst writing this book and wish to thank the following for their time and patience: Mrs Blackett-Barber formerly of the National Maritime Museum, London; Jeremy Farrell at The Museum of Costume and Textiles, Nottingham; Sylvia Hopkins at The National Army Museum, London and Camberley; Elizabeth McCrum at The Ulster Museum, Belfast; and Kay Staniland and Jill Spanner at the Museum of London.

At the Victoria & Albert Museum, there are many colleagues I would like to thank, including Sara Hodges for continuing, with such flair, the splendid programme of photography for this book begun by the late Danny McGrath; and Valerie Mendes, Curator of the Textiles and Dress Department, Wendy Hefford, and Santina Levey formerly of the Textiles and Dress Department. Also thanks to the team at V&A Publications: Mary Butler, Head of Publications, Miranda Harrison, my editor, Geoff Barlow, Production Consultant, and Valerie Chandler, indexer.

Finally, I would also like to acknowledge the generous assistance of Roy Bishko and his colleagues at Tie Rack.

First Cock Sparrow. "WHAT A MIWACKULOUS TYE, FWANK. HOW THE DOOSE DO YOU MANAGE IT?"

Second Cock Sparrow. "YAS. I FANCY IT IS RATHER GRAND; BUT THEN, YOU SEE, I GIVE THE WHOLE OF MY MIND TO IT!"

Introduction

The long tie is such an accepted item of men's dress that few stop to consider its origins. It has in fact taken over three hundred years to reach its present form, and while tracing its development this book will also look at why this rather small item of dress has become such an important guide to a man's identity. Because it has always been seen as an ordinary object, the tie's chances of survival have been slim. Consequently, it is often difficult to provide concrete evidence or examples to illustrate an orderly chronological sequence. The most useful published and original sources used for this book are outlined below.

Sources for the study of ties

Original and complete examples of neckwear from the seventeenth and eighteenth centuries have not survived in significant numbers. Information about historic neckwear can often be obtained from the visual evidence of painted or engraved portraits, contemporary written sources such as inventories and account books, and letters, diaries and contemporary literature. Dictionaries, an increasing number of which were published in the seventeenth century, usually give a brief description of different types of neckwear. These entries, as in the *Dictionaire Universel* (1690) by Antoine Furetiere, are unillustrated. A volume from this period with notable illustrations, however, is Randle Holme's *The Academy of Armory and Blazon* (1688). While portraits show how it was worn and what it looked like, written accounts provide prices and indicate how often and what quality of neckwear was required. This type of information is supplied in detail in *The Expence Book of James Master Esquire* (1646-76). Letters and diaries, such as the *Letters of Lord Chesterfield to his son*

1 *opposite* Tie with concertina pleats of shot silk in gold thread and green silk. Japanese, 1997. By Issey Miyake. T.259–1997

and Others (1739–73) and *The Diary of Samuel Pepys* (1660–8/9), are invaluable as they offer a personal reaction to the fashions and society of the day, as well as describing their own taste in dress. Further useful information can be obtained from biographies and auto-biographies. *The Life of Beau Brummell* (originally published in 1844) by Captain Jesse, for instance, provides a valuable insight into Brummell's sartorial habits, even though the author only met him towards the end of his life while in impoverished exile.

It was not until the early nineteenth century that fine neckwear became an obsession, combined with a growing interest in the etiquette of correct fashionable dress. This resulted in a spate of little booklets on neckwear – or on dress generally – which were usually published with illustrations. These were intended to alleviate a gentleman's problems in tying different knots, and to advise on the appropriate knot for specific occasions. The first of these publications was *Neckclothitania or Tietania, being an Essay on Starchers, by One of the Cloth* (1818). This was quickly followed by *Dress and Address, dedicated to the Merveilleux of Either Sex* (1819), dealing with all aspects of dress as well as cravats. The third, and probably the most influential, was first published in France in 1827: *L'Art de Mettre sa Cravate, par Le Baron Emile de L'Empese*, published in London and New York as the *Art of Tying the Cravat by H. le Blanc* (1828). There were at least seven editions of this book, published in English, French and Italian between 1827 and 1829. Concerned with both men's and women's dress as a whole, but including an entire chapter on cravats, was the *Manuel Complet de la Toilette ou L'Art de S'Habiller avec Elegance et Methode contenant L'Art de Mettre sa Cravat par M. et Mme Stop* (1828). Although the cravat illustrations appear to have been copied from *The Art of Tying the Cravat*, the text is different. The publication of *The Whole Art of Dress, being a treatise…of present day Gentlemen's Costume by a Cavalry Officer* (1830), appears to be the last of these guides to correct dressing. By the mid-nineteenth century newspapers and fashion journals were fulfilling this role.

The increasing number of newspapers and periodicals in the nineteenth century included illustrations of the latest fashions, as can be seen in *La Mode Illustrée*. Another illustrated source, the mail-order catalogue, appeared towards the end of the century. Firms sold everything one could need by this method, including clothing. Sears & Roebuck of America were amongst the first to do this on a grand scale.

Not until the early twentieth century did further books on etiquette and correct dress appear. In North America Emily Post published her comprehensive work *Etiquette* (1922), which included basic information on correct dress for both men and women. C.F. Curtis, an English tailor who published *Clothes and the Man* (1926), offered more specialised information. After the Second World War a book of the same title, written by English tailor Sydney D. Barney, was published in 1951. This followed much the same theme as its precursors but in greater detail. Men's fashion magazines, such as the American publication *Esquire*, discussed accessories with as much zeal as they did mainline fashions. *Esquire's Encyclopedia of 20th century Men's Fashions* (published in 1973) is an invaluable source, spanning the years 1900 to 1973 and including every aspect of men's fashions. The fashion revolution in men's dress in the 1960s is recorded by Rodney Bennett-England in *Dress Optional* (1967). A few years later Nik Cohn wrote about the changes in men's dress since the Second World War in *Today there are no Gentlemen* (1971).

The interest for ties generated in the 1960s has resulted in the publication of a number of books, too numerous to mention here. One of the best known, however, with an introduction by James Laver, is *The Book of Ties* (1968) and looks at school, club and service ties. Richard Atkinson, weavers of Royal Irish poplin and tiemakers, produced in 1970 a useful book about their firm, *Ties are their business*. Tie Rack, which now has outlets in all major cities in Britain and America, published an amusing book on ties and their history, *The Book of Ties*, in 1985. Another delightful book, *Fit to be Tied* (published in the USA in 1987), concentrates on the ties of the 1940s and 1950s.

Since the necktie originated in Europe in the second half of the seventeenth century, the following chapters show the variety of neckwear worn by men (and similar styles adopted from time to time by women) from the 1650s to the present day.

Chapter One

Bands, Cravats and the Steinkirk or Neckcloth 1650–1720s

Bands

Neckwear, because of its proximity to the face, was of prime importance in drawing attention to a handsome or beautiful physiognomy. Those who could afford it could not resist fine neckwear to enhance their appearance and boost their self esteem. Samuel Pepys, who because of his position in the Admiralty moved in aristocratic circles, had a professional need to keep up his appearance and was not best pleased on one occasion in 1663 when, 'This morning, dressing myself and wanting a band, I found all my bands that were newly made clean, so ill-smoothed that I crumpled them and flung them all on the ground and was angry with Jane'.

From the end of the sixteenth century the word 'band' was loosely applied to any neckwear that was not a ruff. It could indicate a plain attached shirt collar, or a detached band that draped over the doublet collar. This latter was known as a 'falling band', and was usually a separate collar that fitted around the neck inside the doublet collar. Randle Holme, in *The Academy of Armory and Blazon* (1688), noted three main sizes: 'A Collar Band, is for the Collar of the Doublet only. A Minikin Band, is of a middle size, not big nor little. A Cloak Band, is so large, that it covered all the shoulders'. The cloak band was a style of the 1630s. Fine examples can be seen in the portraits of *John, Lord Belasyse of Worlaby*, by Gilbert Jackson (1636), in London's National Portrait Gallery; and *Thomas Bruce, 1st Lord Elgin*, by Cornelius Johnson (1638), in Rangers House, Greenwich, London.

A fashionable band of the 1640s, though still wide, fell just short of the shoulders, lying flat on the chest in two broad bibs with squared ends and trimmed with a lace edging of more modest proportions and smaller scallops than those of a decade earlier. In the 1650s the bibs of the band tended to shorten and become narrower. The V&A owns a miniature, dated 1653, by Samuel Cooper (plate 2) which shows an unknown youth wearing a plain linen band, with pendant bandstrings finished with elaborate tassels formed by a tight grouping of decorative knots. It required care and skill to tie the bandstrings so that these tassels were visible just below the band. The bands would have been made of plain linen of the finest quality.

Randle Holme defined bands as 'an ornament for the neck, which is of the finest white linnen cloth, as Flaxen, Holland, Lawn, etc: & is made by the art of the Seamster, and Washed and Starched, Slickened and smoothed by the care of the Laundress'. His emphasis on the maintenance and care of the band, in a work on heraldry, shows the importance of quality laundering, particularly with plain bands which would show every blemish. Besides enhancing the overall appearance, shirts and neckwear were intended to protect the rich silks or woollens of doublets and bodices, which could only be dry cleaned (by scouring with substances like fuller's earth).

Laundry had to be a well planned exercise, and was not carried out every day. All the water had to be fetched by hand to be heated in a copper, and afterwards the washing had to dry, and then be ironed. The disruption of the day-to-day routine was considerable, so it was obviously more economical to do the washing in large batches several weeks apart. Depending on the size of the household, laundry days occurred once every six weeks or more; only the less well-off needed to wash linen once a fortnight or once a week. In 1695 the economist John Houghton wrote, 'I find upon enquiry that in good citizens Houses they wash once a Month, and they use, if they wash all their Clothes at home, about as many pounds of soap as be Heads in the family, and the higher the people be, the oftener they change'. In the Pepys' household, laundry days were usually a month apart, recorded with exasperation or resignation in his diary, 'and so home and the house foul, it being washing day; which troubled me because tomorrow I must be forced to have friends at dinner'.

2 below Gentleman wearing a plain band with tasselled band strings. *Unknown Man*, 1653. Miniature by Samuel Cooper (1609–72). P.121–1910

Two hundred years later there does not seem to have been much change in the process. Flora Thompson's autobiography *Lark Rise to Candleford* (1945) recalls her childhood in the 1890s, and describes a laundry day of the village Post Mistress:

Miss Lane still kept to the old middle-class country custom of one huge washing of linen every six weeks. In her girlhood it would have been thought poor looking to have had a weekly or fortnightly washday. The better off a family was, the more changes of linen its members were supposed to possess, and the less frequent the washday. That was one reason why our grandmothers counted their articles of underwear by the dozen.

This numbering of underwear in dozens has a long history and also applied to neckwear, which was bought in quantities commensurate to the owner's income. In 1697–98 William III in a single purchase acquired 24 flowered neckcloths and 24 cravats. In 1662 Pepys was beginning to spend more money on his clothes, and on 8 October he recorded buying a 'scallop', a lace-edged band:

Hither this night my scallop, bought and got made by Captain Ferrars lady, is sent, and I brought it home – a very neat one; it cost me about £3 – and £3 more I have given him to buy me another. I do find myself much bound to go handsome; which I shall do in linnen, and so other things may be all the plainer.

3 opposite A chart of armorial devices. Bands and ruffs appear in the top row, numbers 1–6. Cravats have been squeezed in at numbers 6, 10 and 54–55. Randle Holme, *Academy of Amory and Blazon* (1688), Book 3, folio 16. NAL; V&A

However, four days later he admitted to 'being loath to wear [my] own new scallop, it is so fine'. By 19 October he had overcome his hesitations, and is referring to his new purchase as a 'lace-band': 'Lordsday. Got me ready in the morning and put on my first new lace-band; and so neat it is that I am resolved my great expense shall be lace-bands, and it will set off anything else the more'.

Bands and shirt cuffs were often acquired together to form a matching set, and were extremely costly in relation to the combined cost of doublet, breeches and cloak. It was the lace which was so expensive. The most fashionable lace in the second half of the seventeenth century was Venetian needle lace, particularly well suited for dress, and for men's bands especially. Motifs were made in various sizes, one of the most enduring being the bold, heavy three-dimensional *gros point* which remained popular until the end of the century. Other finer and more elaborate types included *rose point* and *point de neige*, the finest of all. Whatever the size of motifs in Venetian lace they were all of one design, instantly recognisable with their branching curving stems incorporating leaves and flowers.

In the 1660s the bands deepened at the front and became narrower, projecting forward slightly where they fitted snugly under the chin and over the top of the stiff doublet collar, creating a distinctive soft drape effect. The bib-fronted band continued to be worn, but only on formal occasions and by professional men in the Church and the legal profession. By the eighteenth century bands worn by ecclesiastics and

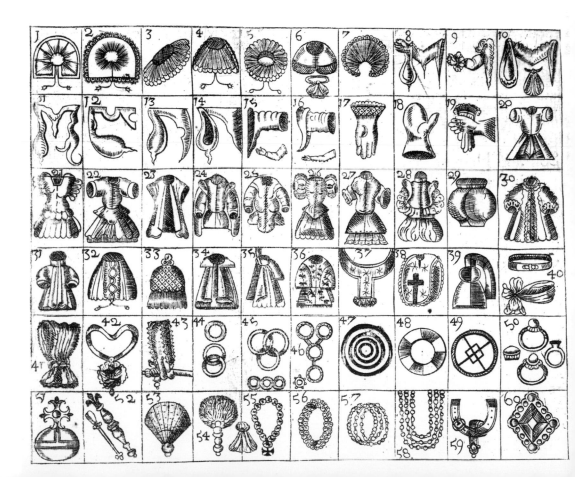

lawyers had become completely stylized. The bibs were reduced to a pair of narrow linen tabs, a tradition that has continued to the present day. Meanwhile fashionable neckwear began to range through many different shapes and styles.

Cravats

When Randle Holme originally prepared the engraved plates to illustrate his *Academy of Armory and Blazon* (1688), he had not allowed space for cravats. Finding himself overwhelmed by the variety of new styles, he squeezed a few into odd places, underneath the original images or crossing the grid separating the coats of arms of a fan and a necklace (plate 3). His definition read:

A Cravatte is another kind of adornment for the Neck being nothing else but a long Towel put about the Collar, and so tyed before with a Bow Knott; this is the Original of all such Wearings; but now by the Art and Inventions of the seamsters, there is so many new ways of making them, that it would be a Task to name, much more to describe them.

His references to a 'long towel' and 'bow knot' are easily understood; the cravat was simply placed about the neck and tied in a bow at the front. Unfortunately he does not offer a description of the other styles, and his drawings are not clear. The one illustrated in plate 3, no. 6, may be intended to represent the simplest form of cravat, where the rectangular towel is held in place under the chin by a silk ribbon. This style can be seen in Samuel Cooper's miniature of Sir Robert Henley, dated 1659 (plate 4). He wears a plain rectangular 'towel' held in place by a cravat string with elaborate tasselled ends. Red and black were popular ribbon colours, but blue and green were also worn. Dictionary definitions of the term appear in the 1650s. In Adolphe Hatzfeld's *Dictionnaire Generale*, published in French in the nineteenth century, 'cravat' is in use in 1652 and given as, 'cravate, an application of the national name Croatian'. In Thomas Blount's *Glossographia* (first published in 1656), he also describes the cravat as a French word, *crabbat*, but then confuses the issue by describing it as 'a new fashioned gorget which women wear'. This definition seems

4 above Early cravat style, with two short ends tied together with a tasselled cravat string. *Sir Robert Henley*, 1659. Miniature by Samuel Cooper. P.113–1910

5 opposite Cravat with the ends tied beneath the bow. James II *c.*1680–90s. Engraved by R. Bonnart. E.21408–1957

suspect, for in the *Glossographia*'s fourth edition (1674), Blount gives a rather different definition: 'Crabbat. Fr. is of late well known with us to be that linnen which is worn about Men's especially Souldiers and Travelling Necks instead of a band'.

The cravat's distinguishing feature seems to be that it is tied in a bow, or is gathered in front by a string or ribbon tied in a bow. This may have stemmed from a military practice evident in 1640s portraits of noblemen engaged in the Civil War in England. A high proportion show the men in buff coats and breast armour (gorgets). Proud, confident and wealthy, they gaze firmly ahead. About their necks they invariably wear a richly laced band, and in the majority of these pictures the band has been caught up under the chin by a ribbon tied in a bow.

The Scottish National Portrait Gallery houses a portrait of Charles II as Prince of Wales, painted by William Dobson c.1643. It shows him

Iacques II. Roi d'Angleterre d'Écosse et d'Irlande
Sur vn peuple muin, j'ai de l'authorite'   Mais je devrois reguer sans crainte
Mon empire pourra souffrir quelque contrainte   Si la valeur faisoit la seurete.

wearing a laced band that has been gathered together by a piece of pale blue silk ribbon, tied in a neat bow. In another portrait by Dobson, Colonel Richard Neville of Berkshire appears to be wearing a military neckcloth of plain linen, with the ends held together with black silk ribbons tied in several bows, or 'knots'. This method appears to have been adopted by the 1650s. The neckwear worn by Sir Robert Henley (plate 4) is a simple neckcloth with the ends tied together by a tasselled band string. The military neckcloth, probably of linen, possibly of silk, was wrapped several times about the neck and either tied in a knot, the ends tucked in at the front or simply left hanging. The ribbon-tied bands or neckcloths may have been the inspiration for the sophisticated ribbon-tied cravats of the 1670s–80s.

By the 1670s the cravat had become a rectangular 'towel' gathered at the front and usually fastened by a prominent silk ribbon tied in a bow. Engravings of James II of England (plate 5) and Louis XIV of France (plate 6) show two methods of tying the cravat with a ribbon. The first shows one or both of the cravat ends just under the bow, whilst the other shows the ends flipped over the bow. Both bows appear to be stiffened and would have been ready-made.

There are contemporary literary sources which offer useful references to ready-made cravats. In William Wycherly's first play, *Love in a Wood* (performed in 1671), it is declared that: 'Twould be as convenient to buy satires against women ready made, as it is to buy cravats ready tied'. Aphra Behn, in her play *The Feigned Countess* (1679), gives this vivid stage direction: 'Petro puts out the candle, comes to Tick, unties his cravat behind and flips his head out of his periwig'.

A rather unusual representation of a cravat dating from this period was that carved in limewood by Grinling Gibbons (plate 7). The carving appears to represent a ready-made cravat, where bow and cravat-ends were an item and fastened at the back of the neck. The lace is finely carved and is recognisable as Venetian *gros point*. James II wore exceptionally fine lace on his wedding outfit (plate 8), and interestingly here too the cravat-ends are of Venetian *gros point*.

The neck stud, an additional decoration to neckwear, made its appearance during the 1670s as the cravat became progressively more sophisticated in style and construction. The desire to have a jewel at the neck has persisted through the eighteenth and nineteenth centuries to the present day. Sometimes neck studs matched rich shirt sleeve buttons or cuff-links of precious metals set with jewels.

Most contemporary portraits and fashion plates show cravats that are of quite modest proportions, but it seems that when made of rich lace they could be very long and, what is more, were apparently tied with a simple slip knot. This stage in the change from cravat to neckcloth can be seen in Van Musscher's portrait of Hendrick Bicker, Burgomaster of Amsterdam (plate 9). His cravat / neckcloth is made entirely of a heavy Venetian needle point, matching that on the shirt front and sleeve ruffles. It is tied in what is probably a slip knot and reaches

6 below Cravat with the ends flipped over the bow. *Louis XIV of France*, c.1680–90s. Engraved by R. Bonnart. E.21397–1957

7 opposite, left Carved limewood cravat. British, 1670s. Carved by Grinling Gibbons (1648–1721). W.181–1928

8 opposite, right Cravat of Venetian *gros point*, 1670s, displayed with the 1673 wedding suit of James II at the V&A. T.41–1947

Le Roy

Iay tout le monde sur les bras   Et j'espere enfin que la france
Sans rien perdre de ma Constance,   Fera tousjours trembler tous les autres Estats.

nearly to his waist. The portrait is dated 1682 – by the 1690s cravats had fallen out of fashion, although they continued to be worn for formal occasions.

Neckcloths: The Steinkirk

As heavy Venetian needle lace declined in popularity in the late 1680s and 1690s, the long lace cravat was replaced by a plain or lightly trimmed neckcloth, a change that was perhaps accelerated by the influence of military dress during the French War of 1689-97. The neckcloth was very simple to wear, being a long narrow piece of linen or muslin tied just once about the neck in a loose knot, with lace or fringed ends. The minimum length for a neckcloth that reached the waist would be about 6 feet (182cm). The muslin neckcloth in the V&A (plate 10) measures 13¼ inches wide (34cm) by 5 feet 11½ inches (152cm) long, including both of the 7½ inches (19cm) laced ends. When the ends were twisted together and tucked into a button-hole (of either a coat or a waistcoat) the neckcloth was called a *steinkirk* or *steenkirk*, which takes its name from the battle of Steenkirk in Flanders in 1692. Since the French defeated the English, the name is most likely to have originated in France. Visual sources show the steinkirk as early as 1693. The dashing gentleman in plate 11 wears a steinkirk with laced ends, tied once about the neck and twisted, with the ends poked through a buttonhole. His whole appearance is of studied negligence. According to Voltaire, the style stemmed from the hastily assumed attire of the French noblemen called suddenly to battle with barely time to adjust their clothing.

The steinkirk proved to be popular with both men and women until the 1720s. As can be seen in fashion plates and portraits of the period, women were prompt in adopting it to wear with their fashionable ensembles as well as with their riding habits. The use of 'steinkirk' to refer to the neckcloth appeared quite early in contemporary literature. In 1695, William Congreve's play *Love for Love* refers to 'Criticks with long wigs, Steinkirk Cravats and terrible faces'. Although the neckcloth had a military background it had also been worn as infor-mal dress with the nightgown. This can be seen as early as 1666 in a

9 opposite Neckcloth or cravat of heavy Venetian needlepoint, in a style that was the forerunner of the steinkirk. *Hendrick Bicker*, 1682. Portrait by Michiel von Musscher (1645–1705). Rijksmuseum, Amsterdam

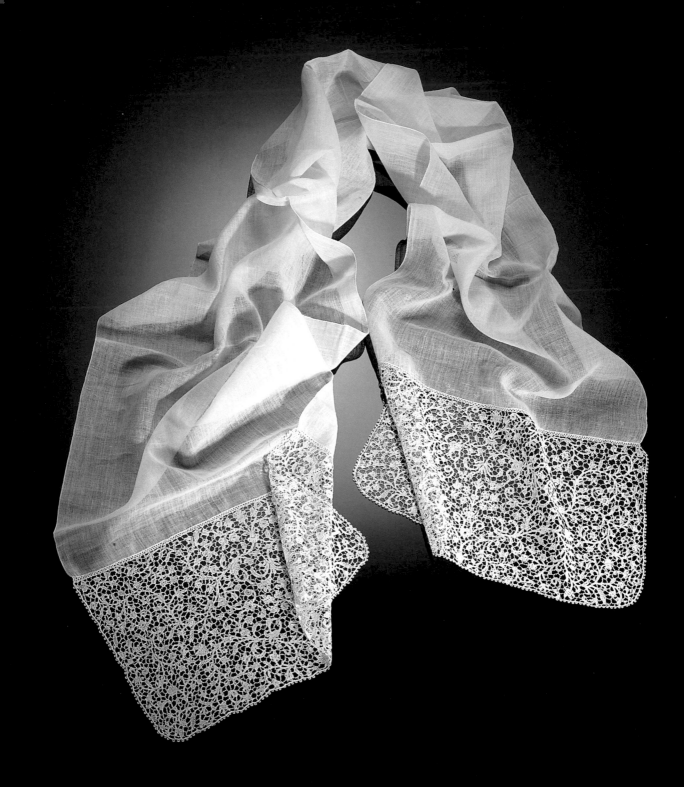

Dessiné par J.D.De S.Iean. 1693.   avec Privilege du Roy.

Homme de qualité en habit garny d'agrémens

se vend a Paris sur le Quay Pelletier a la Pomme d'Or au premier appartement.

10 opposite Neckcloth of muslin, the ends decorated with needlepoint lace. Italian 1690–1710. T.158–1992

11 right French fashion plate showing steinkirk tucked into button hole. *Homme de qualité en habit garny d'ágrémens*, 1693. Engraved by Jean de St Jean. 26363-14

portrait of Samuel Pepys by John Hayles (plate 12). For this painting Pepys wore a plain neckcloth with an Indian nightgown that he hired for the occasion. The neckcloth was probably his own and appears to be of linen.

Material

Towards the end of the seventeenth century lace suffered a decline in favour of fine Indian muslin imported by the East India Company. Muslin had always been everyday wear in place of lace, but the fashionable preference for muslin at the turn of the seventeenth century is confirmed by contemporary inventories, accounts, and portraits. Some neckcloths had fringed ends with fine silk bands woven across, others had additional decoration in the form of a row of stylised flowers or plant forms. These may have been the type which are referred to in William III's bills as 'flowered muslin'. English customs records show a huge increase in imports by the East India Company between 1697 ('To London from East Indies…Neckcloths…2557 @ 4s each') and 1698 ('from E. India…Neckcloths… 20495ps [pieces]').

The plainness of muslin also made it suitable for mourning dress. Antoine Furetiere, in his *Dictionaire Universel* (1690 edition), mentions that a muslin cravat was worn for mourning. Correspondence from the Verney family reveals that two years earlier, Edmund Verney, mourning for his brother, wrote: 'I have made me a new Black cloth suit, and a new black mourning Gown, which with new muzeline Bands and cloth shooes will stand me in very near ten pounds'. The wardrobe accounts of William III record: 'For his Majesties mourning for the late Electorall prince of Bavaria, for 42 yards of superfine muslin at 18s £37 16:00'. This order was for 24 cravats, which allowed about 1¾ yards (169cm) per cravat, allowing for a reasonably large bow knot. The accounts of the seamstress Edith Colledge for 1699–1700 include the following costs for making cravats from muslin:

For making 18 muslin Cravats	2:05:00
For making 18 muslin necks to the Cravats	1:02:06
For making 18 pair of muslin ruffs	2:05:00
For the first washing of the same	1:16:00

12 opposite Plain neckcloth worn with a nightgown. *Samuel Pepys*, 1666. Portrait by John Hayles. National Portrait Gallery, London

The ruffs were not neckwear but wrist ruffles that would have been sewn to the shirt cuff band. By the late seventeenth century the separate deep cuff, which used to be turned back to fit closely over the doublet sleeve, was allowed to drape over the hand in a ruffle.

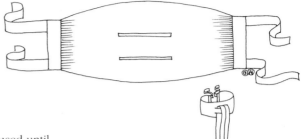

DIAGRAM 2.

Styles of Neckcloth

The single loose slipknot employed for the neckcloth was used until the 1720s. There had also been a transitional style incorporating a stock and neckcloth. The stock was a rectangle of linen gathered at each end onto a narrow band or tab and then fastened at the back of the neck, either with tapes, a button or a buckle (plate 13). The neckcloth was simply folded into a long narrow strip or band, ironed flat and then threaded through either one or two horizontal slits, placed one above the other at the centre front of the stock. Both ends then hung down the front of the chest rather like a necktie. Care was taken to ensure that they were of equal length. An example of this style can be seen on a child effigy in Westminster Abbey dating from 1715 (plate 14). The four-year-old Marquess of Normanby wears a linen stock, with two slits in the centre front so that both ends of the neckcloth, which is of lace, could be slotted through and allowed to hang.

'Tyed' neckcloths are referred to in the inventory of Benjamin Jackson, a mason-contractor who died in 1719. His household and personal linen were all lumped together, and amongst his shirts were 'Ten tyed neckcloths, twelve old ditto'. (Whether the executors meant the type of neckcloth just described, or whether they meant cravats or stocks is impossible to decide, but either way these were ready-to-wear.) The term neckcloth here was probably used to signify neckwear generally rather than a particular style.

In another style a neckcloth could be tied in the usual way and be finished off with large and showy tassels, similar in size and decoration to the tasselled band and cravat strings of the seventeenth century. This style remained in fashion until the 1720s; thereafter it was still worn for sport or informal dress, but the method of tying changed to what we might call a 'muffler' or 'scarf' knot. This was a loose single knot with one end being pulled or puffed out to cover both the knot and the other end.

The changes in fashionable neckwear were not isolated developments, but were prompted by other fashions. Hairstyles had a considerable influence on neckwear, and conversely neckwear could have a profound influence on hairstyles. The starched cartwheel ruffs of the sixteenth century made it impractical to have long hairstyles, but as the ruffs softened, or 'fell', they allowed hairstyles to reach shoulder length. With the introduction of wigs in the late seventeenth century there was no longer any point in having enormous and costly collars or bands. Neckwear became concentrated to the front of the chest, complimenting the length of the full bottomed wig by becoming as long or even longer that the wig's tails. The next chapter will look at how extreme this had to become throughout the eighteenth century before the inevitable decline of the wig.

13 opposite Diagram to show the tying of stock and neckcloth. © A. Hart

14 right Lace neckcloth and linen stock; the neckcloth is folded and threaded through two slits at the front of the stock. Effigy of the Marquess of Normanby aged four, 1715, in Westminster Abbey.

Chapter Two

Stocks, Solitaires, Neckcloths and Cravats 1720–1800

During the eighteenth century, men's neckwear changed steadily. Old names were adopted for new styles, as with the reintroduced cravat of the 1770s. The neckcloth varied in importance but remained in use within certain social groups into the nineteenth century. The ready-made cravat, which coming from the early eighteenth century pre-dated the stock, reappeared in a slightly different form a hundred and fifty years later. This chapter will look at these complex developments chronologically and by type, taking into account the changing meanings of some of the terms.

The Stock and Solitaire

By the time the full bottomed wig had disappeared in the early eighteenth century, the cravat had given place to the neckcloth, stock and solitaire, except for official and formal dress. During the 1720s and 1730s the most distinctive change in neckwear was due to the influence of the bag-wig hairstyle. This was part of a totally new image for men, featuring a neat and clear cut silhouette: the coat fitted to the waist before flexing out into wide and stiffened or padded skirts, and the hair worn shorter and confined at the nape of the neck in a little black silk bag, like a drawstring purse. The neckwear worn with the bag-wig was the stock, which created the effect of a white column supporting the head, as it completely covered the neck and collar of the shirt from jaw to Adam's apple. The stock continued to be worn for formal and full dress throughout the eighteenth century.

The bag-wig is thought to have been derived from the *tye* or *tye-wig*, a hairstyle for sportsmen or soldiers who for comfort and convenience

15 opposite Bag-wig and solitaire. The ribbons of the solitaire are attached to the bag wig and tied in a large bow at the throat. Plate IV, *The Arrest*, 1733–4. Scene from *A Rake's Progress* by William Hogarth (1697–1764). (PP+D)F118(31)

tied back their wigs or hair with a bow of black silk ribbon. To wear a bag or bag-wig, the hair of the wig was tightly curled at the sides and plaited in a pigtail or 'queue' at the back. When the hair was powdered for dress or full-dress occasions, the queue was enclosed in a bag to protect the coat from the powder. The bag was usually decorated with a bow at the top just below the opening. One particular variation of the bag-wig, known as the solitaire, had matching ribbons stitched on either side at the top of the bag: these were then brought around the neck, where the stock was already in place, and tied in a flamboyant bow under the chin. *The Arrest,* the fourth plate from the series of painting and engravings by William Hogarth (1663–1764) entitled *A Rake's Progress* (1733–5), shows the Rake dressed in the height of fashion wearing a huge bag-wig with the ribbons tied in a loose solitaire (plate 15). This style was not usually worn without the bag-wig. Sometimes, however, it was worn as a separate item with the

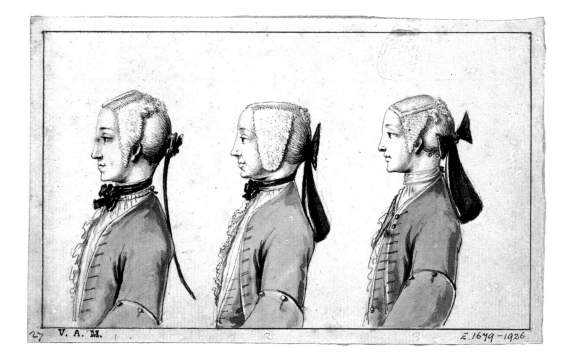

16 opposite Plate showing three styles of solitaires and bag-wigs. Bernard Lens, *The Exact Dress of the Head* (1725). E. 1679–1926

17 below Informal dress consisting of nightcap and nightgown worn over waistcoat and shirt. The shirt collar is open and the ribbon tie undone; artistic licence allows it to be draped across the chest. *George Pitt,* 1720–30. Bust by Henry Cheere. A.7–1983

stock, like a bow tie. Drawings by Bernard Lens (1682–1740) for *The Exact Dress of the Head* (1725) show several variations of this neckwear, where the solitaire is shown as a separate item from the bag-wig (plate 16). *The New Bath Guide* of c.1766 includes high praise for the solitaire:

But what with my Nivernois' hat can compare,
Bag-wig, and lac'd ruffles, and black solitaire?
And what can a man of true fashion denote,
Like an ell of good ribbon ty'd under the throat?

Occasionally a portrait shows a formally dressed gentleman with the solitaire untied and the ribbons free and dangling over his shirt front, in a rather untidy and relaxed manner. It may be presumed that he is easing any discomfort felt from wearing the bag-wig and the rather restrictive solitaire. A good example of this is a portrait of James Bruce of Kinnard, painted by Pompeo Batoni in the 1750s, and now in the Scottish National Portrait Gallery.

Informal dress, that is the wearing of a nightgown, produced another neck-tie in the form of a narrow, black silk ribbon. A portrait bust of George Pitt by Sir Henry Cheere (plate 17) shows him in nightcap and nightgown, with neck-tie ribbon hanging negligently from a buttonhole in the shirt collar. This style was borrowed from boys' dress. There are many portraits from the first half of the eighteenth century that show boys, usually aged between five and twelve years old, wearing either a frilled or plain upright shirt collar tied at the neck with a neat, narrow black silk ribbon. Often the ribbons are untied and have been left dangling for comfort.

Neckcloths and Stocks

Although by the 1720s the steinkirk had ceased to be fashionable, a white or black neckcloth continued to be worn either as daywear or on sporting occasions. It was probably in France that the earliest black stock or neckcloth was worn: French mounted Grenadiers wore black neckwear as part of their uniform from about 1690 to 1720. In England fashionable black neckwear began to appear sometime in the 1750s.

Although at first this neckwear was worn mainly by the younger sporting fraternity, it later became accepted as fashionable attire. Thomas Gainsborough painted a self portrait in about 1759 which shows him wearing a fashionable black neckcloth, tied in a loose knot. In this form it is also to be found as part of military dress, worn by both officers and men, and adopted by many regiments by the 1770s.

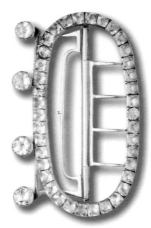

There were at least two methods of tying the neckcloth. It was either tied in a bow like the cravat of the seventeenth century – and could possibly be interpreted as an early revival of the cravat – or it was looped around the neck with both ends pulled halfway through a second loop, creating a loose almost club-shaped knot, with the ends just showing below the knot itself. These ends were fringed or trimmed with lace. To tie the knot successfully a great deal of material was necessary, probably about 6 feet (183cm), the same amount as the old neckcloth.

A formalised and fully regulated uniform for the regiments of the British army was not properly organised until about 1742, when the Clothing Register Book was produced. The British military stocks were varied. Included in the clothing and equipment list of an officer of the 17th Light Dragoons, in 1778, were: 'Two white stocks. One black one. Shoe buckles, knee buckles and clasps'. The 'clasps' were the stock buckles. Another military term for neckwear was *roller*, which may have derived from the slang name given to a bundle of linen or underwear, or it could have come from the word used for a rolled bandage. The Oxford English Dictionary offers several interpretations from the 16th century which are appropriate: one is taken from Turbery, *Faulconrie* (1575): 'on everie side binding them with the linnen rollers'. Presumably these 'rollers' were similar in shape to the neckcloth, especially when folded ready-to-wear.

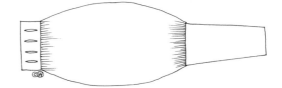

The stock was fastened at the back of the neck, sometimes by a button or tapes, but more usually by a detachable buckle. The buckle was more common as it was easier to adjust and keep the stock firmly in place. Plate 18 shows two silver stock buckles, one of which is set with pastes. Both of them can be dated to about the 1760s. The buckle was attached to one of the tabbed ends of the stock by means of four studs which were inserted into buttonholes (plate 19). The other tab was passed through the buckle and held in place by the prongs.

Richard Nash (1674–1772), or Beau Nash as he is remembered, chose to wear a buckle at the front, where it appears in nearly all of his portraits. The 1742 portrait of him by Benjamin Morris (plate 20) shows a very fine jewelled or paste buckle, very similar to the stock buckle in plate 18. It also reveals that his stock was not stiffened, and that he either wore the buckle there for decoration or in place of a stiffened pad to maintain the shape. Stocks received a lot of wear just under the chin and this method may have helped to preserve them. In 1717 Henry Pelham wrote to his friend, the Honourable George Berkeley, with this request, 'I must trouble you to send me [from Paris] two or three pads for cravats by the first opportunity'. The pads would have been stiffeners for a stock, and could have been of leather or paste board. Whether he was still wearing cravats or simply used the term indiscriminately for either the stock or cravat is uncertain. Later stocks were usually stiffened, especially as they steadily increased in height.

The increased height of the stock of the 1760s meant that the shirt collar had to increase in height as well, having to extend beyond the stock as the shirt was an undergarment, worn next to the skin to protect the stock and other clothing from body oils and grease. Even when wearing a black neckcloth or stock, the shirt collar could be seen quite clearly as a narrow white rim just above it. The excess in material was turned down over the stock, and could of course vary considerably in depth. Some were shallow and stuck out as little points or wings just under the chin, bearing a strong resemblance to the wing collars of the late nineteenth century.

18 opposite, above Silver stock buckles. British, c.1760s. The studs were inserted into buttonholes at one end of the stock, while the other end was passed through the buckle to be held in place by prongs; the remainder passed under the edge of the buckle.
Top: T.12–1980; below: 953–1864

19 opposite, below Diagram to show an early eighteenth-century stock, with its holes at one end and tapered shape the other. © A. Hart

RICHARD NASH Esq. M.C.
Anno 1742.

Cravats

The cravat made its reappearance sometime between the 1770s and 1780s, and its return can be attributed to the fashions introduced by a group that became known as 'Macaroni's', young Englishmen who returned from their European Tour with new ideas on dress which they had seen in Italy. The Macaroni's affected the frilled collar and the fringed or laced cravat that took their name. The *Gentleman's and London Magazine* in 1777 mentioned that 'the Macaronis…[being] the silken ornament worn by way of a cravat, is of such importance to true taste, especially when the knot is elegantly fringed'. It would also appear to be the Macaroni style of neckwear that was adopted by women to wear with their riding habits at this time. These neckcloths, tied in a small bow, could either be trimmed with lace or be made purely of muslin.

One of the fashionable laces at this time was French needle lace, particularly popular for men's dress, usually with a pattern of small floral sprigs, bouquets or spots on a net ground. This modest ornamentation reflected a growing preference for plain fabrics, or at least for minimal patterns. Decoration was becoming more and more restrained as the Rococo gave way to the Neo-Classical style.

The style of any period is of course subject to many influences. Fashions cannot change without reflecting or expressing various cultural or political changes. Here, the purely stylish assumption of classical elegance, with its emphasis on line rather than ornament, stemmed from the interest in classical art which had been stimulated by the earlier discoveries of the Roman cities of Herculaneum and Pompeii in the 1740s. This tendency to plainer dressing also reflected social change – a growing dissatisfaction with the established order of society, building up into a radical storm that was to become the War of Independence in North America and the Revolution in France.

The powdered wigs, elaborately embroidered suits and lace-trimmed shirts and neckcloths of the respectable classes were rejected by some young men, who adopted a slovenly appearance and aggressive manner. They let their hair grow lank and unkempt, wore dirty linen, dressed in their hunting clothes most of the time, and carried

20 opposite 'Beau Nash' wearing a buckle at the front of the stock, where it was both decorative and kept the stock upright. He may have had the buckle custom made. *Richard Nash*, 1742. Portrait by Benjamin Morris. Royal National Hospital for Rheumatic Diseases, Bath

wooden clubs or cudgels. More idealistically, in the second half of the eighteenth century Englishmen from the younger aristocracy, like Charles James Fox, supported the American Colonies in their fight for independence and sympathised with the early stages of the French Revolution. They expressed their convictions by dressing plainly, in clothes usually associated with the merchant and farming classes. All this combined to have a considerable effect on fashion, with the gradual adoption of the riding habit as everyday wear by the 1780s and 1790s. The outfit consisted of a coat, waistcoat, buckskin breeches and boots.

Another country garment to gain respectability and to impact on the development of neckwear was the frock coat. Worn by countrymen since the seventeenth century, it was loosely cut, comfortable to wear, and had a flat turned-down collar known as a cape. Once it was adopted as a fashion garment, during the 1730s, the materials improved in quality and the collar was often faced with velvet. This essentially English fashion was adopted by the French between 1780 and 1790, and French tailors transformed the coat into a high waisted silk version, with wide revers and a high collar. Both the high collar and the revers introduced a definite 'V' neck, necessitating an equivalent high-necked cravat.

Louis-Sebastien Mercier, in his essays *Tableau de Paris*, made the following observations on the dress of young Frenchmen in *c*.1788:

The men wear square-tailed coats with very long waists: the skirts reach the knees; the breeches reach the calves: the shoes are pointed and as thin as paper: the head rests on a cravat as if on a cushion shaped like a wash-basin: or with others the cravat envelops the chin…No more cuffs, no more jabots: very fine linen. A gold pin shaped like a star or a butterfly, shows off the whiteness of the shirt.

The jabot was the shirt frill and not a separate item as is often thought.

In the 1780s and 1790s, neckwear could be plain or coloured. Made of the finest fabric to prevent discomfort the square cloth was folded in half to form a triangle, then folded very carefully several times to create a broad band. The middle of the band was then placed at the throat, the ends taken around the back of the neck and then brought to the front, and tied in a bow. When tied it looked like a cravat, and the two terms were used indiscriminately. A very large square was required, which when folded measured a minimum of 40–45 inches (115cm). A gentleman would have had at least two dozen neckcloths; twelve white and twelve patterned. The recommended number was thirty. The pattern could be of white work embroidery or a woven spot or stripe, and some were trimmed with lace. The Prince of Wales's bills for 1790 show that he ordered 48 white neckcloths of varying types, plus 51 stocks and 30 stiffeners for the neckcloths.

Folding a cravat took on added fashionable significance at the end of the eighteenth century. Men could spend hours getting dressed in the morning, and the greater part of that time was spent in arranging the cravat. The folds had to be just so, and the knot or bow evenly tied. Charles Nodier (1780–1844) recalled when, as a boy in the early years of the French Revolution, he observed Louis de Saint-Just dressing. Saint-Just employed complicated ties for the knots of his cravat, finishing with artistically floating ends. The folds and pleats were then carefully arranged so that the result left his head rising out of a very high cravat, quite unable to move. Following his death at the guillotine in 1794 there was a sale of Saint-Just's effects: his cravats apparently had a value of 1000F and comprised just twelve; six of muslin, five of silk and cotton and one unspecified. The outlandish fops and dandies of the period copied his excessively high cravats, and appeared subsequently for posterity in the contemporary satirical cartoons which lampooned fashions.

Incroyables, Merveilleuses and *Muscadins* were the names given to these French fops or dandies at the time of the Revolution. It was the *Muscadins* who were particularly noted for their enormous cravats (as can be seen in plate 21), which imprisoned the wearer in 'la cravate ecrouelique'. (It is thought that the name *muscadin* might possibly have alluded to their perfume). Of all these groups or factions it was the *Muscadins* who affected subsequent fashions. Their preference for the square-cut frock and tail coat, together with enormous cravats, carried a certain 'street credibility' at the time, which continued to

influence the style of men's dress into the early nineteenth century.

It was at this time in England that George Bryan Brummell (1776–1840), better known as Beau Brummell, began to exercise his influence in high society as the arbiter of good taste in dress. His own taste bordered on the austere, preferring plain dark colours contrasted with pristine linen, combined with an almost obsessive neatness and cleanliness. In one particular portrait, by John Cook, he is wearing an enveloping cravat, similar to those of the *Muscadins*, which would have been wrapped around the neck at least twice and tied in a bow. The effect is one of negligence but it would have been carefully arranged with as little handling as possible.

There are some misconceptions about Brummell's reputation as an innovator. He was mainly a follower of fashion, although he did initiate some changes to dress (such as the introduction of instep or stirrup straps to trousers in order to keep the trouser leg taught and less crumpled). This sort of improvement seems to be typical of his obsession with neat appearance. His considerable influence lasted as long as he remained friends with the Prince of Wales, later George IV. The first rift in their friendship occurred in 1804, and was followed by a final rift in 1813 which resulted in Brummell's exile.

A contributor to the first biography of Beau Brummell (by Captain Jesse) was an anonymous friend who had known him in his heyday, rather than his years of exile and poverty. He recollected that:

He was not a *fop*, as many now think he was: he was better dressed than any man of his day, and we should all have dressed like him if we could have accomplished it. The tie of the neckcloth and the polished surface of the boot-top were then great objects of attention, and no one rivalled him in those attributes.

The book *Neckclothitania* (published in 1818) recommended that 'after the neckcloth is finished, you should pass your finger along the upper ridge, in order to make it lay smooth, and look thin and neat'. Lest he should mark his cravats, Brummell took the precaution of using a discarded shirt to adjust the creases. He was first and foremost a fastidious man, and all his outfits were completed by immaculate linen.

21 opposite Detail of a hand-coloured print entitled *Les Inconcevables*. French 1790s. The *Muscadin* wears a large enveloping cravat with square-cut green frock coat, tightly fitted breeches and bicorne hat. Private collection

His reputation for exquisite neckwear was satirised in a little rhyme:

My neckcloth, of course, forms my principle care,
For by that we criterions of elegance swear,
And costs me each morning, some hours of flurry,
To make it *appear* to be tied in a *hurry*.

Captain Jesse observed:

The collar, which was always fixed to his shirt, was so large that before being folded down, it completely hid his head and face, and the white neck-cloth was at least a foot in height. The first *coup d'archet* was made with the shirt collar, which he folded down to its proper size; and Brummell then standing before the glass, with his chin poked up to the ceiling, by the gentle and gradual declension of the lower jaw, creased the cravat to reasonable dimensions.

To keep them in these carefully structured folds, Brummell's laundered cravats were lightly starched. Once this became known, other men who considered themselves to be dandies copied him, but often went too far and had their cravats so stiffly starched they couldn't move.

However, as will be seen in the next chapter, the basic dress of gentlemen in the early nineteenth century, including dandies, was essentially quite plain and unadorned. Simplicity and modesty were the criteria for fashions adopted by both men and women. The political and social conditions were such that in France plain dressing had sometimes made all the difference between life or death. In England and America there was an instinctive preference for plain simple clothes of good quality. This had been facilitated by the increase in the production of attractive printed cottons and muslins. This style of dress affected all classes of society, and contributed to a certain extent in breaking down social barriers (at least at middle and upper class level). It was Baudelaire who summed up this era so well, explaining that 'Dandyism appears at times of transition…Dandyism is the last heroic gesture amid decadence'.

Chapter Three

Cravats, Neckcloths, Stocks, Scarves, Bandannas and Ties 1800–1850s

Manuals Concerning Neckcloths

The intense interest generated in the tying of a perfect cravat provoked a series of publications, beginning with *Neckclothitania, or Tietania: Being an Essay on Starches, By One of the Cloth* in 1818. The book contained instructions and illustrations on how to tie fourteen different cravats (plate 22). Each 'tie' had a name, to distinguish the difference in the type of knot, including: *Oriental Tie, Mathematical Tie, Osbaldeston Tie, Napoleon Tie, American Tie, Mail Coach Tie, Trone d'Amour Tie, Irish Tie, Ball Room Tie, Horse Collar Tie, Hunting Tie, Maharatta Tie, The Gordian Knot, and The Barrel Knot.*

The book also uses the word 'tie' in association with neckwear, probably for the first time, although it is used to refer to the way a cravat is tied, not as the name of an item of dress. It was published at a time when there was growing interest in men's dress as a whole, most probably because of advances being made in tailoring techniques. There had been a proliferation of books on tailoring in the first quarter of the nineteenth century. *Neckclothitania* is couched in much the same language and uses the same format as tailoring books, complete with appropriate literary quotations on neckwear and dress. It is very small, being intended as a pocket book for easy reference. It seems to have been the first publication in English on neckwear, and had a noticeable influence on subsequent books on the subject. Many appeared within the next ten to fifteen years, often adopting the same quotations and making frequent references to *Neckclothitania*.

Dress and Address and *L'Art de Mettre sa Cravat or the Art of Tying the Cravat* came from the same publisher the following year (1819). In

NECKCLOTHITANIA

Oriental

Mathematical

Osbaldeston

Napoleon

American

Mail Coach

Trone d Amour

Irish

Ball Room

Horse Collar

Hunting

Maharatta

Barrel Knot

Gordian Knot

Way of Folding

G. Cruikshanks fecit

22 left Frontispiece from
Neckclothitania (1818).
NAL; V&A

Paris in the 1820s *L'Art de Mettre Sa Cravat en Seize Lecons* was published by Honore de Balzac (1799–1850), or possibly Emile Marc de Saint Hilaire, under the *nomme de plume* of 'Baron Emile de L'Empese' which was a play on the word for starch. The book ran to a third edition in 1827. This was followed, suspiciously quickly, by an identical publication that same year in English by an 'H le Blanc Esq', followed by a second English edition in 1828 entitled *The Art of Tying the Cravat, demonstrated in sixteen lessons.* The illustrations are identical to the French edition and include thirty-two different styles (plate 23). The author instructs the reader on the care of his neckwear when travelling, suggesting that he provides himself with a box measuring 18 inches (46cm) long and 6 inches (15cm) wide which should contain the following:

1   A dozen (at least) of plain white Cravats.
2   The same quantity of spotted and striped white Cravats.
3   A dozen coloured ditto.
4   Three dozen (at least) shirt collars.
5   Two whalebone stiffeners.
6   Two black silk Cravats.
7   The small iron mentioned in the first lesson.

This seemingly large quantity would probably last the average careful man about two or three weeks, allowing for the laundering to take a week.

In 1828 M. and Madame Stop published *Manuel Complet de la Toilette, contenant L'Art de Mettre sa Cravat, Demontre en 30 Lecons.* They too appear to have plagiarised the publication by 'Baron Emile de L'Empese', although their illustrations are by a different artist. Another English publication, *The Whole Art of Dress* (published in 1830 'by a Cavalry Officer'), includes nine descriptions of cravats and three buckled stocks. The cravats have not changed very radically: the names have been translated here and there, such as *Corsican* for *Napoleon* and *Indian* for *Maharatta*. Indications are that the craze for neckcloths had settled down to a manageable number of styles. The death of Napoleon in 1821 meant that the use of his name for a fash-

Plate A.

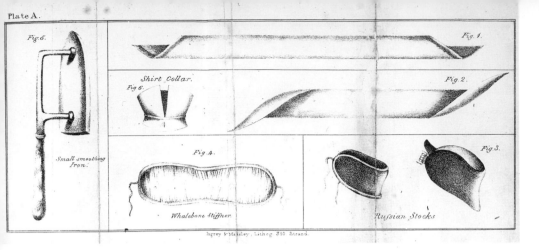

Fig. 5.

Small smoothing Iron.

Shirt Collar.

Fig. 6.

Fig. 1.

Fig. 2.

Fig. 4.

Whalebone Stiffner.

Fig. 3.

Russian Stocks.

Ingrey & Madeley, Lithog. 310 Strand.

Plate B.

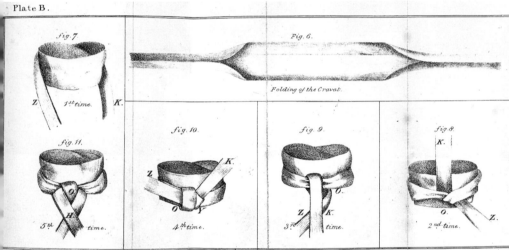

fig. 7.

Z   1st time.   K.

fig. 11.

5th   time.

Fig. 6.

Folding of the Cravat.

fig. 10.

Z   K.

O   Y

4th time.

fig. 9.

Z   K.

O.

3rd   time.

fig. 8.

K.

O.   Z.

2nd time.

Ingrey & Madeley, Lithog. 310 Strand.

Plate C.

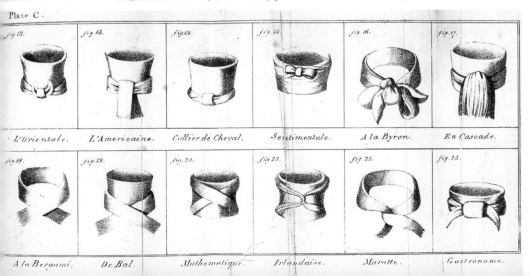

fig. 12.   *fig. 13.*   *fig. 14.*   *fig. 15.*   *fig. 16.*   *fig. 17.*

L'Orientale.   L'Américaine.   Collier de Cheval.   Sentimentale.   A la Byron.   En Cascade.

fig. 18.   *fig. 19.*   *fig. 20.*   *fig. 21.*   *fig. 22.*   *fig. 23.*

A la Bergami.   De Bal.   Mathématique.   Irlandaise.   Maratte.   Gastronome.

ionable cravat had presumably lost some of its immediacy by 1830. The tie in question was simply a folded neckcloth that crossed one end over the other. To hold it in place the ends were tied onto the braces or had tapes attached for tying behind the back. An additional embellishment was a stick, cravat-pin or brooch to pin the cravat to the shirt front. The *Napoleon* cravat was tied exactly the same as the *Ball room* cravat; the difference being that the latter was always white and would have had a more elaborate pin or brooch. The former was for daywear and could be coloured or patterned, worn with more modest jewellery such as a plain gold pin.

The author of *Neckclothitania* made various recommendations in his little volume: he not only gave instructions on how to tie particular cravats, he also suggested suitable colours and fabrics and whether they were better for summer or winter wear. The *Osbaldestone* for instance is a good tie for the summer because, 'instead of going round the neck twice, it confines itself to one. The best colour is ethereal azure'. In the chapter entitled 'Hints' he advises that, 'Neckcloths should always...be made of ribbed or checked materials, as it makes far better ties than when the stuff is plain. Muslin makes beautiful ties, especially for evenings'. With regard to the all important art of starching, *Neckclothitania* contains some interesting observations which have become unfamiliar to us today:

When a starched neckcloth is brought home from the wash, it will be immediately seen that, one side is smooth and shining, the other more rough: this is occasioned by the one side being ironed, and the other not. I do it myself, and consequently recommend it to others, that the rough side, should be worn outside during the day, but, that on putting on a cloth for the evening, the smooth side should be the visible one.

There is a very similar tie which could have been the one known as the sentimentale, which appeared in *The Art of Tying the Cravat*, illustration number 15 (plate 23c), although the book was published much later. The advice given by the author is quite stringent: 'if your physiognomy does not inspire sensations of love and passion, and you should adopt the *Cravate Sentimentale*, you will be a fair butt for

23 opposite Plates from *The Art of Tying the Cravat* (1828). Plate A: The folding method in fig.1 is recommended for the large bow knot of A la Byron, seen in plate C. Fig. 2 shows the ends folded in opposite directions to avoid flopping when tying. The Russian stocks in fig.3, according to the author, always fasten at the back and have plain fronts. To make the stiffener in fig. 4, between 50 and 60 short narrow slivers of whalebone were slipped into as many vertically stitched pockets. Flexible enough to go round the neck, it was rigid enough to keep the chin up. The iron in fig.5 had to be kept clean and glossy. Plate B: Figures showing the folding of the cravat to tie the Gordian knot. Plate C: Drawings of twelve types of cravat knots.

ridicule'. After recommending that only the young and boyish should wear this particular style, the author continues: 'It must be strongly starched, and fastened with a single *rosette* at the top, as near as possible to the chin. It is more fashionable in the country than in town. Cambric is generally preferred'. Despite the advice given by these authors, it seems unlikely that all of these variations were worn. Judging from the portraits of the period the easiest ties were preferred, and about two or three types were used on average.

Black Stocks

The black stock and cravat were made popular by George IV (reigned 1820–30), eclipsing the white cravat except for evening and formal dress. Black neckwear formed part of military dress, and the king's fondness for the black stock can probably be attributed to his interest in uniforms. Although he never served in a regiment, in spite of being made Colonel Commandant of the 10th Light Dragoons in 1793 by his father, George III, he was fascinated by the military. The black velvet stock named *The Royal George* was a style adopted by him in 1822. Efforts to re-introduce the white cravat by William IV (reigned 1830–37) proved to be unsuccessful. After all, the success of black neckwear in either form may simply have been the practical advantage of not showing the dirt. Following his exile and subsequent poverty, Beau Brummell wore black neckcloths for this reason.

Only three black stocks are described in *The Whole Art of Dress*: *The Royal George*, the *Plain Beau* and the *Military*. Of these, *The Royal George* is probably one of the most luxurious pieces of neckwear. Made of the richest black Genoa velvet and satin, with the satin sloping down each side of the velvet to the centre 'with a very handsome tie representing the gordian knot, with short broad ends', they were made all the more noteworthy due to the fact that 'His Majesty and his royal brothers were always remarkable for wearing them extremely high on the cheek, so that the sides

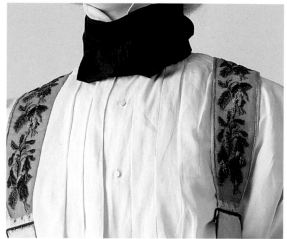

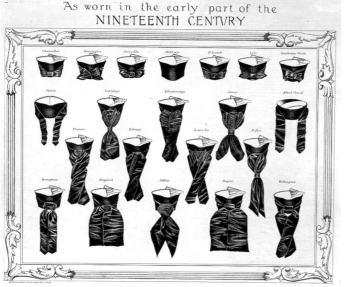

As worn in the early part of the
NINETEENTH CENTURY

And manufactured by
WELCH, MARGETSON & C°., LONDON.

24 opposite Black satin stock. British, mid-nineteenth century. T.122–1963

25 above Illustration of stocks made by Welch, Margetson & Co. in the nineteenth century. Private collection.

came close under the ears, extending to the utmost verge of the chin…The rage for it has passed away and is now deemed singular'.

There is a record dated 1832 of a black silk stock costing 8 shillings. Since no other information was given, it must have been a relatively plain stock, similar to the following description for the *Plain Beau* (or *Bow*): 'nearly straight sided, very pliant, and composed entirely of black silk, with a common bow in front…its appearance is unassuming and business-like. Fashion decidedly Oriental'. The third stock, *The Military*, 'is remarkable for its plain stiff form, which is composed of corded silk, edged with kid and lined with crimson; unlike the two former fashions it has no tie'. The author then notes that the stiffened lining should be of a 'thick whitey-brown leather, which is beaten into shape upon a proper block, it should then be of so unyielding a nature that no force of the neck can bend it'. A stiffener of durable quality could last quite a long time, as it could simply be re-covered whenever the silk had worn out or become dirty or greasy. Another type of stiffener was quilted, like one of white cotton in the collection of costume at the Museum of London. This was surely much more comfortable to wear and was probably used with the hand-tied cravat, slipped inside the cravat when it was folded.

These three stocks were fastened by buckles or hooks at the back of the neck. The most popular style appears to have been that with a bow at the front. These can be seen in many portraits of the period, and quite a number have survived. Plate 24 shows a ready-made stock with a bow-tied knot, made sometime in the 1840s.

Black silk stocks remained fashionable throughout the 1830s, '40s and '50s. Portraits of the period, whether drawn, painted or a photograph, invariably show men wearing a black stock. It is not always possible to discover if they were hand-tied or ready-made. Those that survive are all ready-made. Welch Margetson and Co. published a chart of 21 different stocks that would have been fashionable in the 1840s and '50s (plate 25). Of the three styles already mentioned in *The Whole Art of Dress*, only the *Military* stock remains. One other earlier style may have survived as *The Joinville* (not to be confused with the *Joinville* necktie with fringed ends illustrated on p.73). These stocks, like their cravat predecessors, are given names with a contemporary significance such as *Wellington* and *D'Israeli,* or the *Albert Cravat* (in spite of its name this last is still a stock, and is shown in plate 26). The *Albert Cravat* and the *Opera* both have hanging ends which are intended to be left untied, reminiscent of the undone solitaire ribbons of the eighteenth centure. The *Osbaldestone* continued to be a favourite despite new knots, as a number of portraits from the mid-nineteenth century reveal.

Ready-made Versus Hand-Tied Neckwear

Despite the fact that an increasing amount of neckwear was ready-made, the preferred types were still hand-tied. Ready-made ties were disdained by those who moved in society or were at all fashion conscious, so rather like today there was a considerable amount of snobbery attached to the type of tie worn. This provoked derision from the satirists who could score several 'hits' at once, as in the cartoon from *Punch* in 1853, forming the frontispiece to this book. The drawing mocks, first and foremost, the enormous size of the cravat style that had become popular from the late 1840s, while at the same time poking fun at the difficulty in tying a tie, as well as identifying the social class of the young man by deriding his mannerisms of speech.

Hand-tied knots can usually be recognised if the knot is loosely tied; they are often common knots or bows which first appeared in *The Art of Tying The Cravat* and then in *La Toilette* (both 1828): one is a tie named *Colin* and the other *la Byron*. Both ties became the preferred choice for artists and musicians.

26 above Albert cravat. British, 1850–60s. By Ludlam. T.320–1989.

The Scarf

Another favourite form of neckwear was the scarf, where a necker-chief or bandanna was held in place by slipping the ends through a finger- or scarf-ring at the neck instead of using a knot. This method may have been adopted from the neckwear of sailors. Any of these styles that required only the simplest knot, or no knot at all, must have been much more comfortable to wear and, moreover, easier to fasten.

The National Maritime Museum in London has three unusual scarf-rings made from tropical nuts (looking not unlike small, rounded horse chestnuts). The dome-shaped tops are inlaid with silver metal motifs of an anchor, a star surmounting a heart, and an eagle above a shield. All are associated with Horatio, Viscount Nelson (1758–1805). They measure approximately $1\frac{1}{8}$ inches (3cm) in diameter, with a very narrow slit cut horizontally through the centre to take the scarf. This suggests the scarf would probably have been of silk, lawn or muslin: nothing more bulky could have passed through such a narrow opening.

There are several ready-made scarf-ring styles amongst the Welch Margetson stocks, for example *Jersey*, *Polka* and *Cantilupe*. These are admittedly very elaborate and not at all like those worn with a simple scarf-ring. The fashion for wearing the scarf-ring had become increas-ingly popular by the second half of the nineteenth century. Manufacturers of such small items, or 'toys' as they were known in the trade, had submitted a variety of patterns for scarf-rings to the patent office by the 1860s.

Shawl or Scarf Cravats

Nineteenth-century fashions gradually became more conservative, at least as far as formal daywear was concerned. Any changes were subtle, and largely to do with developments in tailoring. Colours were muted compared to the eighteenth century. Splashes of colour, however, were possible with waistcoats and neckwear, and the combinations of colours and fabrics for the 1820s and '30s had a rich-ness that had not been exploited in quite such a manner before. Fashionable daywear consisted of a frock coat and tight trousers with stirrup straps, worn with a shawl waistcoat, which had a deep shawl collar (so named because its continuous rolled collar gave the appearance of wearing a shawl, or perhaps in reference to the shawl fabrics and patterns that were a popular choice for waistcoats at the time). This also applied to the name for the scarf or shawl cravat fashionable in the 1830s and 1840s (plate 27). The cravat was so extensive that it required the restraint of a cravat pin to hold it to the shirt front. These items of male jewellery became very elaborate, consisting of a long pin with a decorative head, plus one or more fine chains. The caricature of Count d'Orsay by Daniel Maclise (plate 28), drawn in 1845, shows him wearing a superb glossy black satin shawl cravat.

Another full-fronted style was the *Mail-coach* or *Waterfall* neckcloth. *The Whole Art of Dress* explains that, in order to create the desired 'waterfall' effect, the cloth has to be extremely large and free from starch: 'The tie is made by folding the cloth loosely round the neck and fastening it with a common knot, over which the folds of the cloth should be spread, so as to entirely conceal it…Colour generally white, but not unfrequently various'.

The wedding cravat in plate 29 is a fine example of an Osbaldestone (see plate 22, top row).

The Last of the Dandies

English men's dress and fashion were influenced by such personalities as Beau Brummell, Lord Byron, Lord Lytton and Count d'Orsay, as well as prominent followers of fashion such as the young and ambitious Benjamin Disraeli, and Charles Dickens. They were all contemporaries, although not of the same generation, and by definition belonged to that group of elegant men known as dandies, a fashionable phenomenon closely linked with the Regency period. At his most extreme the dandy was mocked for his effeminacy and vanity in dress and behaviour. Lord Lytton, better known as Bulwer-Lytton, wrote one of his most successful books about the Regency period and the cult of the dandy, *Pelham*, published in 1828. This was in fact a witty and tongue-in-cheek critique of the period.

Dandies were becoming an extinct species by the 1830s, however,

27 opposite Black satin
shawl cravat. British, 1840s.
T.215–1966

28 right Caricature of Count
d'Orsay wearing a shawl
cravat. The *Frasierian
Magazine*, 1834, pl.146.
Drawn by Daniel Maclise
(1806–70). NAL; V&A

and Count d'Orsay (1801–52) was considered by his contemporaries to be the last. Compared to Brummell, who epitomised an angular austerity in his dress, d'Orsay could be described as sinuously luxurious: he reintroduced the curve. Jane Welsh Carlyle wrote, in 1839, of an unexpected daytime visit from d'Orsay, 'all resplendent as a diamond-beetle [with] sky-blue satin cravat'. His neckwear was frequently described as 'glossy', and 'filling' the shirt front. Wearing this style in sky-blue it is no wonder that people commented, for it was an extremely eye-catching piece of neckwear, especially if he also wore a jewelled gold cravat pin and a few chains as well. For evening dress he sometimes dispensed with neckwear altogether and just wore diamond studs at the collar of his shirt.

Collars and Shirts

Most of the neckwear described in this chapter required a high shirt collar, which in the early nineteenth century measured on average about 5½ inches (12.5cm) deep. The points were even higher and were nicknamed 'winkers' or 'ears'. Shirt frills had also become stiffly pleated and very deep, so that they protruded from the chest giving the effect of a pouter pigeon or, as Washington Irving described them in 1823, like 'the beard of an ancient he Turkey'. A change in shirt styles began in about the 1820s, at least for daywear, when the frill was left off and pleats were introduced down the front. This was not an absolute change: frills simply became optional, and were always worn for evening dress. The depth of the opening remained the same, being about 12 inches (30.5cm), but was provided with plain linen buttons, where hitherto it had been left open. Shirts were always pulled on over the head, and never opened all the way down the front. Buttoned openings invited the use of decorative or jewelled buttons or studs as well as shirt brooches. This was greatly encouraged by the open-fronted styles of the waistcoats after the 1820s.

The great rolled coat collars, so fashionable in the 1820s and '30s, gradually diminished in height from the 1840s and '50s onwards. Consequently shirt collars became lower, restricted to being upright bands, but still retained points or 'wings' (or were simply turned

29 above Pink satin Osbaldestone. British, 1840s. Museum of Costume and Textiles, Nottingham

down). Cravats and stocks, in keeping with this development, became narrower and less bulky, even ribbon-like as in the Byron tie, described in *Punch* in 1842 as 'small ends of silk commonly called remnants, and sold at eighteen pence each'.

Neckties and Cravats

The lowering of the shirt collar proved in retrospect to have a significant effect on the style of men's neckwear. From the mid-nineteenth century there was a distinct change not only in the size, but also in the style of cravats and stocks. No longer could a man wear a rigidly stiffened and buckled stock or a neck-throttling cravat. A low narrow collar demanded an equally narrow necktie. From this period onwards, the term 'necktie' can be applied to these narrow bands tied in either a rigid or a floppy bow. The term 'cravat' was loosely used for any form of neckwear. The low collar stimulated the introduction of a variety of neckties, for not only were they made of colourful silks but the manner of tying them varied considerably. Yet whether they were hand-tied or ready-made, the knots were the basic bow knot, the reef knot or the sailor's knot. Neckties referred to as 'once-around ties' appeared: the *Punch* cartoon of 1853 (frontispiece) shows that these huge bow ties were actually worn.

Other ties that made their appearance were the *Octagon*, a ready-made tie, and the *Ascot*. These were probably derived from early examples of knots published in *Neckclothitania* and *The Art of Tying a Cravat*. However, Welch Margetson also offered a confusing range of styles, from which the stylised *Octagon* and *Ascot* could have developed. There was still a degree of snobbery about ready-made ties, an attitude that survives in the twentieth century. Sydney Barney in his booklet *Clothes and The Man* (1951) includes this warning amongst his 'do's and dont's' for the well-dressed man: 'avoid wearing a bow tie with a stiff double collar. This indicates the bow is ready-made'.

It was possible to indicate social position by the choice of collar and tie. C.W. and P. Cunnington wrote:

the elders have collars with points onto the cheeks, worn with a swathing neckband or 'Napoleon', and these commonly have the upper two or three buttons of the waistcoat gaping. Artists and writers lean towards the low double collar, which Mr Dickens wears with a vast satin cravat and pin, and Mr Millais wears a hanging necktie knotted through a ring. By such idiosyncracies a gentleman was able to indicate his personal attitude to life while marking his position in the community – He wore so to speak a label round his neck.

The colour of a tie could also be used to indicate the wearer's political persuasion. Towards the end of the nineteenth century, socialists had adopted the red tie as a political badge. It was worn by 'artists and writers and some men sufficiently high born to be able to ignore the conventions'. This convention is still upheld by the British Labour politician Anthony Wedgewood Benn who is 'practically never seen without a red tie to proclaim where he stands in politics'.

Alison Lurie observed in her book, *The Language of Clothes*, that at any one time there were differences in style across the continent of America, with specific styles being associated with particular areas: for instance, in the Deep South men's dress suggested not only the southern gentleman but also the dandy, whereas in the mid-west the men preferred comfortable sporty clothes and 'their striped or foulard ties will be brighter and patterned on a larger scale than those purchased in sober New York and Boston'.

The combination of a narrow tie and slippery starched collar presented a problem for the wearer, as the tie would not stay in place. This encouraged the invention of a variety of ingenious methods to anchor the tie. The simplest of these took the form of several unobtrusive flat hooks. Attached to the bottom of the inside neck band of the tie, these were then hooked under the lower edge of the detachable shirt collar.

Ties continued to be splendid, affording the wearer an opportunity to show his taste (or lack of it) in his choice of pattern and cravat pins. Although the stiffened stock went out of fashion, men had not escaped from the restraints of starched collars. In the 1850s and '60s these were relatively low, but as the century progressed collars rose until they were high as the jaw, and as restricting and uncomfortable as the neckwear worn between 1800 and the 1840s.

Chapter Four

Neckwear for Riding and other Sports: the rise of the 'Old School Tie'

As has been noted earlier in this book, simpler, more practical forms of neckwear tended to be adopted for hunting and other sporting activities. This was also the area in which women had begun to adopt male fashions, something they continued to do during the nineteenth century. Plate 30 gives a good idea of the diversity of neckwear for outdoor pursuits. Many of the neckwear styles were available as ready-made ties or cravats. The fashionable stock with bow tie at the front was the most popular, and was made in a number of different colours as well as in black and white. (A white stock was reserved for evening dress, whereas black and all other colours were acceptable for day and riding dress.) It was at this time, and specifically for sporting activities, that the changing shape of neckwear made possible its use as a means of group identification. These rather specialist aspects of the tie are addressed in this chapter.

Women's Riding Dress

In her memoirs of 1800 Susan Sibbald wrote of setting off in a coach with her father, where she recalls that both of them wore habits with lapels 'which when open displayed waistcoats, frilled shirts, stand up collars and black silk handkerchiefs around our necks'. The similarity of her habit to men's dress was so marked, she said, that they could have been mistaken for two youths. Military fashions were also adopted for women most successfully, with jackets and collars often richly decorated with braid. At the turn of the century some jackets had upright close-fronted collars, the height of which meant that

30 left Summer Fashions for 1838, View in Windsor Park. By B. Read. From left to right: The gentleman in the foreground wears a white stock with a bow; the gentleman facing him wears a brown stock decorated with blue birds and tied in a bow with flowing ends. Behind him Queen Victoria, on horseback, wears a cravat that resembles the *coquille,* while her companion and a man in the centre background wear white stocks with bows. On the far right in the background, a gentleman on horseback wears a black waterfall or *mail coach* neckcloth. In the foreground two gentlemen wear different types of stock, one black with a large floppy bow, the other white with a small bow. The boy on the right wears a black silk bow, the other has a neckcloth or handkerchief tied in either a reef knot or *A la Colin.* Guildhall Library, Corporation of London

no cravat was required. The military style and braided decoration persisted throughout the nineteenth century.

However, from the 1820s softer styles, consisting of a falling collar worn with a black stock, were introduced. This reflected the current fashion for wider, open necklines in women's dress, accentuated by the increasing size of the gigot sleeves. By the late 1830s a neat round collar was worn with a high buttoned corsage and finished with a ribbon cravat attached by a brooch. The collar and tie were not unlike the neckwear of boys at this time. These ties were knotted with what appears to be a 'common' knot, which may have been a reef knot judging by the way the ends point away from each other.

There were several variations to riding habits of the 1840s; some consisted of a corsage with the collar and lapels like a man's coat, buttoning to the waist. Alternatively the corsage fastened at the neck with a small turned-down collar, or remained open with a habit shirt and buttoned down the front. A black cravat was usually worn with these fashions.

Sporting Clubs

Racing has long been referred to as 'the sport of kings'. It was also the first sport to adopt 'colours' in order to identify the jockeys by using the distinctive colours of liveries. This use of colours spread to distinguish other fashionable sporting groups.

The interest that developed in sport in the second half of the nineteenth century, and particularly the last quarter, was the result of an increase in the leisure time and prosperity of the middle and working classes. These circumstances provided a social setting that accepted women not only as loyal supporters, but also as active participants. The time was ripe for the development of sporting clubs and societies, which included new sports such as cycling and lawn tennis.

The sports that fashionable people participated in were mainly equestrian, namely racing and hunting. In Europe and America different hunts had established their own choice of colour for their riding dress in the eighteenth century. Most of the famous English sporting clubs were founded in the nineteenth century. Whether for angling,

Club Colours.

All the leading Club Colours.

31 above Club ties of silk for I Zingari Cricket Club. Colour plate from the Welch Margetson menswear catalogue for 1908, p.120. T.712–1997

32 opposite The I Zingari Cricket Club (I. Zingari C.C.) and the Marylebone Cricket Club (M.C.C.) are included in this page from a club ties sample book. British, 1950s. James Edwards Ltd, Manchester. T.200–1993

CLUBS

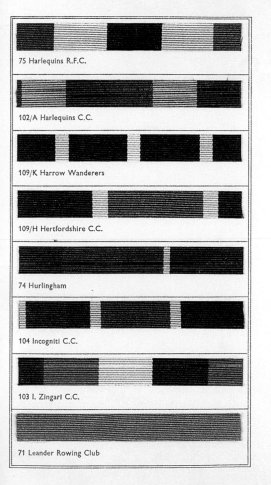

75 Harlequins R.F.C.

102/A Harlequins C.C.

109/K Harrow Wanderers

109/H Hertfordshire C.C.

74 Hurlingham

104 Incogniti C.C.

103 I. Zingari C.C.

71 Leander Rowing Club

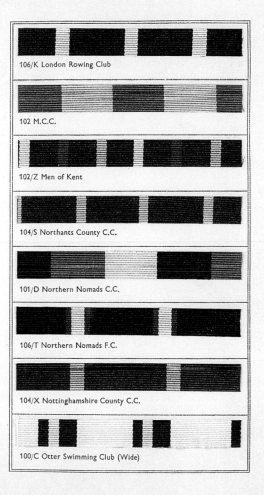

106/K London Rowing Club

102 M.C.C.

102/Z Men of Kent

104/S Northants County C.C.

101/D Northern Nomads C.C.

106/T Northern Nomads F.C.

104/X Nottinghamshire County C.C.

100/C Otter Swimming Club (Wide)

LONDON HOSPITALS

REGIMENTS

LONDON REGIMENTS

shooting, rowing, cricket or football, sports became organised into recognised competitive groups or clubs. James Laver, in *The Book of Ties*, points out that the earliest recorded set of sporting colours belongs to the I Zingari Cricket Club. Founded in 1845 by a group of Cambridge men whose leisure pursuits included cricket and amateur theatricals, its famous colours of black, red and gold symbolised 'Out of darkness, through fire into light'. They were originally displayed on the flag flown over the pavilion during matches. When they came to adopt a tie (in the 1870s), it obviously incorporated the same colours. Plate 31 shows one of the club ties manufactured by Welch Margetson.

Club ties began to make a wider appearance in the late nineteenth century with the growth in the foundation of sporting clubs. As seen above, one or two well established clubs already had colours and badges. The evolution of the flat long tie coincided with the growing popularity of sporting clubs; its shape proved to be peculiarly well suited to display the boldly coloured stripes and bands chosen to represent individual club colours. The introduction of club ties gave a completely new purpose to neckwear, supplying a need to wear a 'badge'. This need rapidly expanded to include schools, universities, the services and other institutions, and as a consequence benefited tie and silk manufacturers. A sample book from the Manchester firm of James Edwards, dating from the 1950s and now in the V&A collection (plate 32), provides not only a fascinating glimpse of the variety of designs produced by this company, but also of the types of institutions who commissioned Edwards to produce their colours.

Schools, Universities and the Services

Initially the introduction of colours to symbolise something arose from the universities and public schools, whose 'House' colours or badges were worn for house matches. In the mid-nineteenth century boys at Rugby School wore jerseys (rather like sweatshirts) with their house badge on the front. At Eton too, the schools had their own distinguishing colours, which were eventually applied to caps, ties, socks, scarves and so on. New & Lingwood, suppliers to Eton College

33 opposite Handmade printed silk tie, with Eton College colours cap motif. British, 1996. By New & Lingwood. T.259-1997

since 1867, stocks a range of especially created handmade silk ties, the designs of which each signify an important aspect of Eton life (plate 33).

The need to identify with a group also spread into the services, so that eventually both the army and the navy (and later the Royal Air Force) devised ties woven to their specifications incorporating their colours and badges. Provision of these became a vital part of the business of silk manufacturers such as Richard Atkinson & Co. Ltd of Belfast, Northern Ireland (established 1820), and Vanners Silks Ltd of Sudbury, Suffolk, England.

Daywear and Sporting Ties in the Nineteenth Century

Ties worn during the day or for watching sport could be very colourful and tied in a variety of knots, whether hand-tied or ready-made. A 'sporting' tie refers to one worn by the sporting fraternity rather than by sportsmen. Sporting ties of the early nineteenth century were quite often made of printed cottons, or from imported dyed Indian silk squares that used the wax-resist technique for their patterns. A very well-known type of neckcloth was called the 'Belcher', named after James Belcher (1781–1811) the boxer, whose fondness for the colourful Indian silk neckcloths made them fashionable amongst the sporting fraternity of the day. Belcher is shown wearing one with a stylized floral pattern, in the portrait of him painted in about 1800 (plate 34).

The 1819 publication, *Dress and Address*, poked fun at the young dandy or beau who wore the sporting style of dress:

The bang-up Ruffian we've so often seen
In light topp'd boots, which take a day to clean,
With under-waistcoat, and with morning frock,
Of form half-hunter's, and broad brim on block,
With fist of pugilist and brownish hue,
Though Ruffian paints and wears the boddice too.
The Osbaldeston or the mail-coach tie
Of cravat, strikes the tip-top Blowings' eye-
The Belcher handkerchief when out of town,
Or to his snug and kennel driving down.

The printed cotton neckcloths were large squares which, when folded in half, diagonally measured between 45 and 50 inches across (114–127cm). Decoration was usually around the edges of the square and might have a sporting theme of horses, dogs or hunting. These prints were very fine and the motifs very small. Other neckcloths were just woven or printed checks or stripes on a white ground, much like men's handkerchiefs of today (plate 35). These neckcloths were often very colourful and worn by flamboyant characters. Great care was taken to co-ordinate the colours of the clothes around the neckline. The neckcloth was precisely tied in the desired knot and the ends tweaked to either cover or reveal the shirt front. The waistcoat, and sometimes one or more slip waistcoats (visible sections made of a fancy textile, the rest of plain linen or cotton), were chosen to form

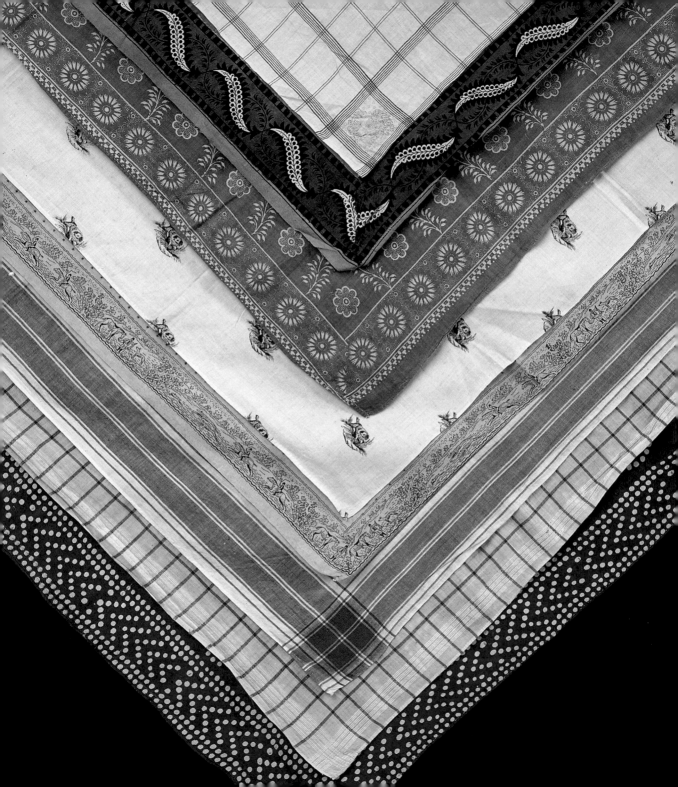

35 opposite Group of eight nineteenth-century neckcloths, showing the borders. From the top: (i) white printed cotton with red stripes, dog's head motif printed in purple in each corner; (ii) block printed cotton, beige ground, purple border; (iii) printed cotton, blue resist ground, floral repeat around border; (iv) white printed cotton, dog running through grass printed in purple; (v) printed buff cotton, fox hunt printed in purple; (vi) white cotton with woven borders in two shades of mauve; (vii) white cotton with woven red stripes forming checks, raised white bands around borders; (viii) silk, wax-resist with blue ground, Indian for the western market.
T.424–1985; T.418–1985; T.422–1985; T.419–1985; T.417–1985; T.416–1985; T.421–1985; T.423–1985

36 above Gentleman's dress from the late 1820s/ early 1830s, showing how coat-collar, Indian silk neckwear, slip waistcoat and lapels were all part of a carefully co-ordinated whole.
T.1738–1913

either a discreet line or a blaze of colour inside the neck opening of the coat. Plate 36 shows the style some young men would have achieved in the late 1820s / early 1830s. A colourful printed Indian silk neckcloth and a pale blue silk slip waistcoat have been placed worn under a cinnamon coloured wool coat with a fashionable velvet shawl collar.

For equestrian or other sporting activities the hunting or waterfall cravat was also still worn. R.S. Surtees describes, in *Mr Sponge's Sporting Tour*, the care taken by Mr Sponge in selecting his cravats and neckcloths for his sporting occasions:

Thus if he wore a cream coloured cravat, he would have a buff-coloured waistcoat, if a striped waistcoat then the starcher would be imbued somewhat of the same colour and pattern. The ties of these varied with their texture. The silk ones terminated in a sort of coaching fold, and were secured by a golden fox-head pin, while the striped starchers with the aid of a pin on each side just made a neat unpretending tie in the middle, a sort of miniature of the flagrant flyaway, Mile End ones of aspiring youth of the present day.

On closer acquaintance with Mr Sponge it becomes increasingly evident that he is in fact a delightful rogue, the nineteenth century equivalent of the 'wide boy' or 'spiv', and this is reflected in his taste in dress. At the beginning of the hunting season, 'his neck was enveloped in the ample folds of a large white silk cravat, tied in a pointing diamond tie, and secured with a large silver horse-shoe pin, the shoe being almost large enough for the foot of a young donkey'.

To recap, sporting ties, because of their flamboyance, were not considered suitable as fashionable dress and were only acceptable at either a sporting event or when out of town. *The Tailor and Cutter* of May 1895, describing the fashions in ties, stated that 'the tendency still appears to be in the direction of bright and strong colours and designs. The very latest in foulards is a colour called "New Petunia". It is very suitable for boating, race meetings, and similar outdoors dress'. One of the producers of this particular tie was Messrs Welch Margetson.

Chapter Five

Bow Ties, the Scarf or Neckerchief, the Ascot and the Long Tie 1860–1940s

It was during the second half of the nineteenth century that the necktie became an established item of men's dress. Neckwear, whether hand-tied or ready-made, was gradually evolving through four distinct styles. They were given a great many different names which can be confusing. For the sake of clarity they will, for the moment, be given names that are familiar: (i) bow tie (ii) scarf or neckerchief (iii) Ascot and (iv) four-in-hand or sailor's knot, generally referred to as the 'long tie'. Certain styles were adopted for particular occasions; for instance the scarf fastened with the scarf ring and the long tie using the slip knot were worn for daywear and informal dress. The Ascot was worn for formal daywear or for hunting, when it was usually white. The bow tie could be worn for both day or evening dress, but only black or white were worn for evening dress; colours were reserved for daywear.

Ties worn for daywear became very colourful in the late nineteenth century. This must have been some form of compensation for the sombre colours of suits fashionable at the time. Max Beerbohm, referring to his dress in 1896, said 'my toilets knocked 'em all silly. On Sunday, flannel coat, white waistcoat, purple tie with turquoise pin, duck trousers and straw hat'. The colour for men's everyday dress in town at the end of the nineteenth century was usually black. The reason for this was partly due to the rigorous attention paid to mourning dress, and partly to the convention that gentlemen dressed formally for business. A conservative style generally accepted for town by the end of the century consisted of black silk top hat, black morning or frock coat and striped trousers. Waistcoats and neckwear offered the gentleman and his tailor a chance to introduce some colour.

The *Tailor and Cutter* of March 1895 referred to ties and scarves being the 'saving touch from the monotony of somberness…what our transatlantic friends call neckwear. Bows, scarves and ties seem to get more and more varied, and, in the majority of styles prettier and more artistic'. The same article also referred to window displays of ties: 'A really well arranged tie window is a picture scarcely surpassed for beauty, variety and brilliance of colour…it is no uncommon thing to see a group of ladies…admiring the richness and delicacy of the colours and the artistic draping and arranging of the various shapes and shades'. Some idea of the colours and patterns available for the summer season was also listed:

Mock Clans, a tying scarve in a great variety of extremely bright colours. Light taffetas in stripes and checks…for better class modes large squares with spot on fancy pattern backgrounds…Some of these with white or red spots on a black check ground…Special all silk long scarves are also very much in demand and are largely taking the place of the recently popular 'Windsor'. These run at 21/- dozen. A chintz pattern novelty at once striking and original, and looks very well made up.

Although good quality ties continued to be hand-knotted, during the nineteenth century ready-made ties became widely accepted. Most consisted of a neckband, piece of card or even elastic, that fastened under or near the knot. This and the pair of blades were made separately and attached by various methods. In later more sophisticated forms, the ready-made bows or knots were attached to one end of the neckband, which had a tapered and stiffened end. This was pushed under the knot, pulled through a spring catch, and secured by a pin attached to the back of the knot.

Bow Ties

At the end of the nineteenth century there were at least two distinct styles of bow tie – the Butterfly and the Batswing. The Butterfly was the earlier style, tied in a wide bow with broad ends and a small knot (plate 37); the Batswing was narrower with square ends. This style is

No. XXV.

KNITTED BOW TIE, BUTTERFLY SHAPE, WITH FLEUR-DE-LIS SPOTS.

Materials :—1 oz. Pearsall's Navy Blue " Empress" or "Extra Quality" Knitting, and 1 oz White "Pamela" Crochet Silk. 4 Needles, No. 17 or 18.

CAST on 70 stitches, and knit 6 rounds plain blue.

7th round.—Knit 13 blue, 1 white, repeat to end of round.

8th round.—1 white, 11 blue ; ❖, 3 white, 11 blue ; repeat from ❖ 3 times, then 2 white.

9th round.— Same as 7th round. *10th to 15th rounds.*— Plain blue.

16th round.—6 blue, 1 white ; ❖, 13 blue, 1 white; repeat from ❖ 3 times, then 7 blue.

17th round.—5 blue, 3 white ; ❖, 11 blue, 3 white ; repeat from ❖ 3 times, then 6 blue.

18th round.—Same as 16th round. Repeat from 1st to 9th round.

One round plain blue ; then decrease 1 stitch at the beginning of the 1st and at the end of the 3rd needle, and continue to decrease thus in *every round* until there are only 36 stitches on the needles.

N.B.—*The Instructions apply to Pearsall's Silks only.*

37 above Butterfly bow tie. Plate XXV, *Pearsall's Illustrated Handbook for Knitting in Silks* (1904). Private collection

38 opposite Batswing style of bow tie. Plate XXI, *Pearsall's Illustrated Handbook for Knitting in Silks* (1904). Private collection

known as the 'club bow' in America (plate 38). The *Tailor and Cutter* stated in March 1895 that, 'The Butterfly Bow tie has not quite gone out as has been stated. It has certainly been modified into what is now known as the batswing bow tie, but the effect is practically the same and is attained with much less trouble as a butterfly must be made in proper sizes to fit different sizes in collars'. (The height and width of the butterfly 'wings' would have affected the shape of the collar opening if it was a turned-down collar).

The shape of the Butterfly bow tie illustrated in Pearsall's silk knitting patterns of 1904 (plate 37) has distinctive thistle-shaped or bulbous ends of equal length. Welch Margetson and other firms called their Butterfly bows 'thistle' ties, which is certainly a more accurate description of the shape. The Batswing also has ends of equal length, but they are quite straight, without any shaping (plate 38). Both styles are still worn today.

Bow ties can be worn on both formal and informal occasions. Traditionally the black and white versions are for formal eveningwear. White is reserved for formal full dress, a tradition that had its origins in the early nineteenth century. For daywear, however, the most brilliant colours and flamboyant shapes could be – and still are – worn. Sydney Barney in his guide to men's dress, *Clothes and the Man* (published in 1951), offered this advice for a suitable informal outfit that consisted of a very conventional beige suit with some startlingly bright accessories:

Suit, Two piece light fawn Prince of Wales check…

Shirt, soft with double collar,

bow tie, of red foulard with yellow spots

Slipover, yellow

Socks Yellow

Shoes Brown suede

Hat Tweed type pork-pie.

The bow tie was also a popular style in America, reaching a peak of popularity in the 1930s. *Esquire* magazine described several outfits which included the bow tie; all were quite different with varying pat-

No. XXI.

KNITTED BOW TIE, STRIPED DIAGONALLY IN THREE COLOURS, OR PLAIN.

Materials :—One ¼ oz. of Pearsall's "Empress" or "Extra Quality" Knitting Silk in each Colour. 2 Needles, No. 18.

Note.—A *applies to the upper colour*, B *to the middle and* C *to the lower.*

1st row.

CAST on 2 stitches colour A.
  2nd row.—Purl.
  3rd row.—Knit 1, make a stitch, knit 1, make a stitch.

  4th row.—Purl.
  5th row.—Knit 1, make a stitch, knit 2, make a stitch, knit 1.
  6th row.—Purl. Continue making 2 stitches every

N.B.—*The Instructions apply to Pearsall's Silks only.*

39 opposite Clip-on bow ties. French, 1920s. Private collection

40 right, above Bow tie. British, 1960s. Made by Turnbull & Asser. T.362–1979

41 right, below Silk bow tie. British, *c.*1983. Designed and hand-painted by Hugh Dunford Wood for Blades of Savile Row. T.89–1985

terns such as polka dots, stripes and plaids. Those bow ties featured in plate 39 are French, dating from the 1920s.

The polka dot design for the bow tie has continued to be popular. In the late 1960s, during the Pop and Op Art periods, both the long tie and the bow tie proved to be a perfect article of dress for adopting some of the most imaginative and outrageous designs, combined with the most flamboyant colour combinations. The firm Turnbull & Asser (of Jermyn Street, London), noted for its traditional high-class menswear, produced a very cleverly designed 'op art' bow tie, composed of two strongly contrasted polka dot patterns (plate 40).

Sydney Barney points out that 'More than by any other single item of clothing the choice of a tie or bow expresses the character of the wearer...[Neckwear] should not distract from the face, and because it is the most prominent item of clothing it must always be carefully presented...Avoid novelty, they are made for those who depend on the tie for conspicuity'. He would have found it difficult to come to terms with fashions since the 1960s, for these rules have been deliberately broken. However, he would not have found fault with the painted pink silk bow tie by Hugh Dunford Wood for Blades of Saville Row, London 1982/1983 (plate 41). This tie was selected to go with a suit by Blades.

The vivid Op Art bow ties were an example of ties that can only be worn by a person possessed of considerable self confidence, something generally needed to wear a bow tie during the day. It could be argued that men can be divided into two groups: those who do and those who don't wear bow ties. Angus McGill, in an amusing article about the bow tie, described it as a 'garment that combines confident flourish with absolute respectability'; although he also claims that once he puts on a bow tie he instantly becomes 'as bumptious as bow-tie wearers everywhere'.

Scarf or Neckerchief

One of the most popular forms of scarf or neckerchief was the 'De Joinville'. It was named after the Prince of Joinville who visited England in 1843 and introduced a knotted scarf with laced or fringed

42 opposite Five styles of neckwear. From left to right: Flowing End Teck scarf; De Joinville scarf; Puff scarf; Famous de Joinville scarf; Four-in-hand scarf. Page 222, Sears & Roebuck catalogue (1897)

ends, which spread across the shirt front without the ends crossing over each other. R.C. Surtees' character Lord Scamperdale wore a 'once-round Joinville' at its most extreme: 'He had been eminently successful in accomplishing a tie that would almost rival the sticks farmers put on truant geese to prevent their getting through gaps or under gates'. By the late nineteenth century, De Joinvilles were either knotted or secured with a scarf ring. They were also available in a shaped ready-made form. The *Tailor and Cutter* noted: 'a rich light long scarf of the kind the Americans call "Joinvilles" [is] specially worth of attention'. A few years later the Sears & Roebuck catalogue for 1897 described the De Joinville as 'the most popular and swellest gentleman's scarf ever produced'. It continued, 'These scarfs are 6 inches wide and 38 inches long, and are made from the purest woven silk…[of] blue, lavender, light green, cherry, strawberry, olive, myrtle, moss green, turquoise, opal red…with light contrasting shades of cream, white, bright shiny yellow, pale blue'. It is only possible to guess at the patterns described: 'brocade patterns in Persian effects, Oriental effects, Dresden fancies, Chameleon grotesques, Roman

43 left Ascot cravat. Figured satin. British, 1870. T.37–1948

44 below Ready-made Ascot. Plate IXX, *Pearsall's Illustrated Handbook for Knitting in Silks* (1904). Private collection

45 opposite Sailor's Knot tie. Plate XVIIB, *Pearsall's Illustrated Handbook for Knitting in Silks* (1904). Private collection

To form an opening through which to draw one end of the tie, work 1 group, 2 D.C. into the next hole, and 2 chain, 2 D.C. into every hole until within one of the end, into which work 1 group as usual and turn.

Work 1 group, 1 D.C. into the last chain of last row. Make a chain of 27, and finish the row with 1 group as usual. Turn, and work 1 group into the first hole and 1 group into every third stitch of the chain (in the same manner as at the commencement of the stock);

N.B.—*The Instructions apply to Pearsall's Silks only.*

novelties, Scotch and Highland checks, and an almost endless variety of artistic and fashionable designs'. The illustration in the catalogue shows a De Joinville worn with an ordinary finger ring (plate 42, second from the right).

The Ascot

Still worn today, the Ascot first appeared in the 1890s. Superficially it resembled an earlier ready-made tie, the Octagon. This was developed in the 1860s and took its name from its knot, which could be rotated for use in eight different positions, thus spreading the wear and tear. The folded cloth of the flat knot suggested that the ends were crossed over the shirt front but, as they would have been completely hidden by the high buttoned fashionable waistcoats of the day, the tie probably only consisted of a neck band and knot.

The Ascot, which could be ready-made (plates 43 and 44) or tied with a simple knot, had square-ended blades that were crossed over the shirt front and held in place with a cravat pin. Its basic measurements were 50 inches (127cms) long, the neck band 7/8 inch (2cms) wide, and each blade 15 inches (38cms) long by 3 inches (7.5cms) wide with closed square ends.

The Sailor's Knot and the Four-in Hand Tie

Identifying the sailor's knot is made difficult by the number of names it has been given over the past 100 years. 'Sailor's knot' appears to be the original term, and was followed in the 1870s by 'four-in-hand' and then by 'Teck', an American tie introduced in the 1890s. ('Teck' only applied to ready-made ties which were identified by their wide and usually square ended blades; see plate 54).

It was during the 1830s and 1840s that the sailor's knot appeared, when the tie became part of the fashionable dress of women and children. It is not clear from descriptions whether the sailor's knot is a slip knot or a reef knot. A slip knot is distinguished by the triangular shape of the knot and ends that hang down straight, one on top of the other. This is achieved when the tie is folded flat and interlined. (Interlinings were introduced in the 1860s.) A reef knot has a completely different

No. XVIIʙ.

KNITTED SAILOR'S-KNOT TIE (NARROW), IN DOUBLE KNITTING, STRIPED OR PLAIN.

Materials:—If Plain, 1 oz. Ball Pearsall's "Extra Quality" or "Empress" Knitting Silk. If Striped, ½ oz. Ball in addition of the colour stripe desired. 2 Needles, No. 18.

(*This Tie is about 1¼ inches wide.*)

THE directions below are for horizontal stripes, but if the Tie is desired plain, the stripes can be omitted, *i.e.* the rows in colour B should be worked with colour A.

Cast on, in colour A, 30 stitches. Double knitting is worked as follows:—Silk in front, slip 1, silk back, knit 1. This is repeated throughout. Work 6 rows colour A, 1 row colour B, 2 rows A, 1 row B, 2 rows A, 1 row B. It must be remembered that in double knitting, a forward and backward row count as one. Work in these stripes for 18 inches. To decrease for the

N.B.—*The Instructions apply to Pearsall's Silks only.*

appearance, having a lumpier knot which lies on its side with the ends pointing away from the knot. Both appear to have been adopted as fashionable knots for ties and both can be correctly called 'sailor's knots'.

The slip knot used for the modern long tie is quite definitely called the 'sailor's knot' in some knotted tie patterns of 1904 (plate 45). Confirmation of this knot being worn as part of a sailor's uniform can be seen in plate 46, a photograph taken in c.1854 of a boy of about fourteen years old in sailor's dress, showing him wearing a recognisable sailor's knot tie tied in a slip knot. An officially approved uniform for petty officers and seamen was established in 1857. The uniform regulations of 1892 stipulated the following neckwear for Chief Petty Officers: 'Class I: Working Dress. Handkerchief – Black silk made of half a Service Silk Handkerchief cut diagonally across, tied in a sailor's knot'. A similar regulation applied to officers who were expected to wear the sailor's knot for everyday dress.

In her book *Victorians Unbuttoned* (1986), Sarah Levitt illustrates a number of ready-made ties that were registered at the Patent Office, one of which, 'The Sailor' cravat, was registered in 1873 by Robert Sayle of Cambridge. This is tied in a slip knot and trimmed around the edges with blue braid on a white cotton ground. The two ends hang down side by side, not one on top of the other.

Another example, this time as part of a lady's riding habit, can be seen in a painting of Queen Victoria in 1838 by Sir Francise Grant (1803-78). She is shown wearing a broad open-necked turn-down collar, with a loosely knotted black neckcloth tied with what appears to be a slip knot or 'sailor's knot'. This seems to be one of the earliest recognisable examples of its use. It is probable that this knot was introduced into riding or sporting dress before it became accepted as fashionable neckwear.

The introduction of a sailor's knot into fashionable neckwear may originate from this period. In 1846 Prince Albert Edward, then aged five, was painted by Winterhalter wearing the ratings uniform of the Royal Yacht (although his handkerchief appears to be knotted in a 'bight' rather than a 'sailor's knot'). The success of this painting led to

46 above Seaman's dress showing the neck-handkerchief tied in a sailor's knot. *Joseph Edwin Moore, c.*1854. Photograph taken when he was about thirteen; he was a seaman between *c.*1854 and 1865. National Maritime Museum

a very popular fashion for little boys. It may have drawn attention to the different, yet attractive forms of neckwear adopted by seamen. It could be another instance where children's fashions have influenced adult styles. The fashion was long-lived and continued until the twentieth century, being adopted for girls as well as boys.

The sailor's knot or slip knot was already familiar as a fashionable tie knot by the 1860s. In a French fashion magazine, *La Mode Illustrée, Journal de la Famille* (1868), there is a page devoted to different styles of neckwear which are all labelled cravats (plate 47). Four of the twelve examples are shown with the 'sailor's knot'. All are ready-made: the descriptions provide very basic information for making up a tie. Unfortunately they do not provide details of how to tie the knots, nor are the ties given individual names. Readers are simply referred to the drawings, on the assumption that they will recognise the knots and be able to reproduce them without any difficulty.

One of the ready-made sailor's knot ties is described as a 'Cravat of striped white and mauve satin'. The cravat is cut from a double length of fabric 9 inches (22cms) and 2½ inches (7cms) from the point and attached to a stiffener. The overall length of the tie, when knotted, should have been about 12 inches (30.5cms). The fabrics selected for the ties were of satin, taffeta, crêpe de chine, repp, and faille. Apart from black and white, the other colours were brown, violet, and sky blue.

All the sailor's knot ties shown in *La Mode Illustrée* were attached to a triangular stiffener with rounded corners. The triangle was inverted so that the widest edge was placed at the neck. It was held in place by a cord attached at one corner, which had a loop that fastened over a small hook on the other corner. The bottom of the stiffener also had a small loop that would fit over a shirt button. This provided a snug fit and prevented the tie from working loose when worn. Plates 48 and 49, a ready-made tie from 1871, show that the stiffener was covered in the same fabric as the tie as the top edge on either side of the knot was partly visible. The early examples of the 1860s and 1870s were fastened under the knot by a spring catch and retaining pin.

Bretelles pour homme.

(TRICOT.)

Ces bretelles, qui s'élargissent vers les épaules, sont tricotées avec du coton blanc sur des aiguilles d'acier; les pattes sont également tricotées. On travaille en *allant* et *revenant*, seulement avec deux aiguilles, toujours à l'endroit. On monte 28 mailles, et l'on tricote de la façon suivante : la première maille est toujours *levée* sans être tricotée, puis alternativement une à l'endroit, — une levée (on *lève* comme si l'on voulait tricoter la maille à l'envers; le brin reste *devant* la maille). Tous les tours suivants sont faits de la même façon, mais la maille *levée* est tricotée à l'endroit, la maille tricotée est au contraire levée. On fait ainsi 50 tours; *deux* aiguilles

CRAVATE EN SATIN SULTAN.

CRAVATE EN SATIN RAYÉ BLEU ET BLANC.

représentent l'un de ces tours. Dans chaque 13e tour (c'est-à-dire à intervalles réguliers de 12 tours depuis le premier), on fait un jeté *après* la première et *avant* la dernière maille, pour élargir la bretelle; ces jetés sont ensuite tricotés en biais comme une maille. Quand on a 96 mailles sur l'aiguille, on continue la bretelle jusqu'à ce qu'elle ait la longueur voulue, jusqu'à sa moitié. La seconde moitié est faite comme la précédente, et l'on y forme les boutonnières. L'autre côté transversal est attaché à une boucle, et l'on y fixe aussi les pattes à boutonnières tricotées comme les bretelles.

Bretelles pour jeune garçon.

(CROCHET.)

CRAVATE EN SATIN RAYÉ NOIR ET BLANC.

CRAVATE EN SATIN RAYÉ MAUVE ET BLANC.

CRAVATE EN SATIN GRENAT.

DESSOUS DE LA CRAVATE EN SATIN RAYÉ MAUVE ET BLANC.

CRAVATE EN FAYE VIOLETTE.

présente la moitié. Pour former la boutonnière du bord in on exécute chaque moitié isolément jusqu'à la hauteur pour la boutonnière, puis on travaille sur toutes les mail augmente sur les côtés, suivant les contours du patron cadre le plastron terminé avec le tour suivant : " une mail ple sur une maille de lisière, — 1 picot, c'est-à-dire 4 en l'air, et dans la première une maille simple, — une simple dans la même maill sière; — on passe une maill sière. On recommence toujou puis ". On répète ce tour à un distance du bord supérieur dessin). On fait de la même sur 15 mailles, deux bandes 70 centimètres de longueur. A bout de chaque bande on form boutonnière; puis on fait di drement (laine noire) pareil

CRAVATE EN TAFFETAS BLEU ACIER.

CRAVATE EN SATIN RAYÉ BRUN ET BLANC.

CRAVATE EN REPS NOIR.

CRAVATE EN CRÊPE DE CHINE BLANC.

du plastron; on c les bandes avec percaline grise; forme des bouton solides sous cell dessus, à 23 centi de distance du transversal inf des bandes; on a celles-ci au pla comme l'indique le sin.

Plateau

POUR SONNETT

La figure 60 (*verso*) app à cet objet.

On prend le cou d'une boîte en ca ayant environ 9 cen tres de diamètre; recouvre à l'ext avec du velours n l'envers avec du p noir glacé; le dess couvercle est garni disque en carton, vert de velours ayant la circonfé de la sonnette. Le tour du couvercle bordé de feuilles en rouge et drap blanc coupées, d'après la f 60, brodées au

ARRANGEMENT DE CRAVATE.

let. On l'exécute au crochet tunisien *croisé*, avec de la laine zéphyr rouge. Le crochet tunisien *croisé* diffère de l'autre en ce que, dans le premier rang de chaque tour, on relève une bouclette d'abord dans la seconde maille,

russe avec des soies de toutes couleur, et posées de à croiser d'un centimètre l'une sur l'autre; une b

47 opposite French selection of differing styles of cravats. *La Mode Illustreé, Journal de la Famille*, 20 December, 1868, p.403. NAI : V&A

48 right Ready-made four-in-hand tie. British, 1871. T.194–1964

49 below Reverse of plate 48. The stiffened end (top right) is pushed down inside the knot and held in plate by a spring catch, the knob of which is clearly visible.

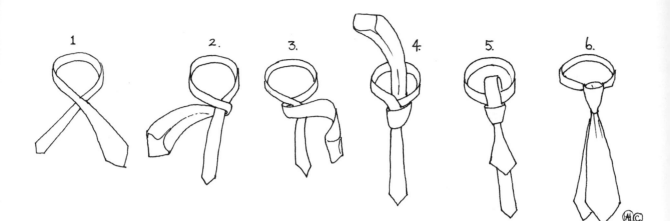

Four-in-Hand Knot

The alternative name of 'four-in hand' was in general use at the end of the nineteenth century and was applied to the long tie using a slip knot, now worn throughout the world. The *Tailor and Cutter* of June 1896 confirms this: 'Four in hands will share the favour of the people as always'.

The four-in-hand is thought to be a reference to the Four-in-Hand Club, founded in England in the nineteenth century by young men who indulged in carriage racing and who adopted this type of knot for their ties. Alternatively, it could refer to the type of knot used to hold the reins of four horses or, more simply, it could derive from the fact that the tie was made from a square folded four times. The early cravats only required four folds on the bias if they were made from a square and, when folded, had pointed ends. If one of these cravats was folded in the usual way but tied in a slip knot, the result would be a tie with very full, wide blades with uneven points and a loose triangular shaped knot. It would have been transformed into a 'flowing end four in hand', as described by the *Tailor and Cutter* in 1896.

Plate 50 shows the distinct stages required to tie the four-in-hand. Sarah Levitt (*Victorians Unbuttoned,* 1986) tracked down an early patent of such a tie, noting that: 'a beautiful sky-blue silk tie, the first to be machine stitched, was registered by Lloyd and Attree in 1862'.

50. Diagram to show the tying of the four-in-hand. © A. Hart

The Long Tie

The basic features of today's long tie evolved from a four-fold cravat of the nineteenth century, the only difference being that now the ties are flat because they are cut to shape and joined on the bias at the centre of the neckband, and have linings and interlinings. The stiff gauze interlining referred to in *La Mode Illustrée* (1868) may only have been recommended for making ready-made ties, for it would not have been a sympathetic material for a hand-knotted tie.

Many of the ready-made sailor's knot ties of the late nineteenth century have a distinctive flat and angular appearance to the knot. This indicates that there was probably an interlining of stiffened material. An important improvement was made between 1920 and 1930, when a piece of bias-cut woollen cloth was introduced for the long tie. The soft yet pliable nature of the wool improved the knot's appearance, giving it a pleasing bulk. It also stopped the blades twisting out of shape.

Another development of the 1920s and 1930s was in the method used to secure the lining and interlining once the tie had been folded into shape. This varied from one manufacturer to another, but the basic principle was to catch the layers loosely together. If the stitching was too tight the fabric would pucker and spoil the set of the tie. The Royal Irish poplin manufacturers, Richard Atkinson & Company of Belfast who have made ties since the late nineteenth century, claim in *Ties are their business* to have introduced the slip stitch for this purpose in the late 1920s. Their poplin ties are:

woven so that the rich silk warp is the visible surface to both sides of the cloth. In the middle of the cloth is the fine worsted weft...The fabric is cut on a true bias and is ultimately folded into a tie which has an all wool interlining, again cut on the bias. The whole is held together by one stout thread applied as a slip stitch throughout the length of the tie. This slip stitch works extraordinary well, except when occasional dullards turn back the end of their tie, and notice the thread, and thinking it a loose one either rip it out or cut it off.

In 1934 the magazine *Apparel Arts* gave a complete description of the construction of the hand-made tie in twelve stages. The seventh described slip-stitching: 'in this all-important operation the main seam which forms the tube of the tie is completed. Resilient construction is dependent upon loose, even stitches sewing lining to back'. Nowadays this method is employed by all tie manufacturers. The same article reiterated the importance of wool as a lining, stating that it determined 'not only the shape of the tie, but its life'.

The cutting of a hand-made tie is done on the bias with a knife 'against heavy cardboard patterns. The large and the small ends are cut one next to the other in reversed positions'. From the 1930s until the 1970s ties were made in two pieces. They are now made in three pieces. A high-quality tie can be cut on the bias from about half a metre. The joins occur in the narrowest section of the neck band.

Collars, Tie Clips and Frames

It has already been mentioned that the height of the shirt collar affected the size and style of a tie. A considerable variety of collar styles were fashionable in the second half of the nineteenth century (plate 51): some were upright, known as 'all-round' collars and with and without wings; others were turned down; some were stiffened; others, as on flannel shirts worn for informal dress, were soft. The opening at the neck also varied: some met at the front forming a rigid band: others left a little V-shaped gap to allow for the Adam's apple. Turned-down collars tended to be shallow but could have a deep turn-down with a wide cut-away at the front.

The upright collars first appeared in 1853-4 and created a fashion for narrow bow ties. Some became so narrow that in 1854 *Punch* remarked that the tie was, 'not half so broad as a watch ribbon. You will be wearing your shoe-strings for a necktie next'. The wide cutaway turn-down collars or the wing collars, on the other hand, encouraged ties with a wide flat knot or the folded Octagon and Ascot styles that became increasingly fashionable in the late nineteenth century. Fashionable men of the late nineteenth and early twentieth centuries usually wore the high upright collar. This style caused problems keeping the neckband of the tie in place

The catalogues of Welch Margetson in the early twentieth century

51 right Four late nineteenth-century visiting cards. A: Upright all-round collar, striped Butterfly bow tie. B: Wing collar, ready-made sailor's knot.
C: Turned down collar with cut-away front, ready-made sailor's knot. D: Upright collar, ready-made Ascot. Private collection.

advertised a range of ingenious accessories which claimed to solve the problem (plate 52). One that was probably most successful was The Royal or Gem scarf retainer, which was a heart- or leaf-shaped wire clip (not unlike a paper clip) plated in gold or silver. The heart-shaped part slid under the base of the collar, leaving an upright stalk on the outside which was finished with a knob curving forward at the top and holding down the neckband of the tie. At least two were needed, one on each side of the knot, and so they were sold in pairs.

Other gadgets were tie frames, which were linked to the development of the ready-made tie. Welch Margetson patented one called the Tymaka Spring Wire Tie Frame, which could be used with the double or turned-down collar for a sailor's knot or for a bow tie. Another device was the Duplex Tie Frame for use with a soft collar. The tie could be folded onto the frame and then fixed into position on the collar by means of two studs on the frame. Yet another, called the Clutch tie frame, also included the collar stud.

Ties and Textiles

Ties were still referred to as cravats in men's dress catalogues of the early twentieth century, and the different types of tie were distinguished by the fabrics used for them rather than by name.

The shape of the tie which used the sailor's knot came in three different styles in the late nineteenth and the early twentieth centuries. One tie, made from a lightweight printed silk square (foulard), was simplicity itself. The method of folding followed the same principles as the cravats of the early nineteenth century. It produced a short tie with wide blades of equal width which, when worn, spread across the shirt front. This created a rather thick neckband and was only suitable for the upright collar.

The long tie was made so that either both points were of equal width with open ends, or the front blade was wider than the back. The neckband was narrower and stitched so that it could be worn with double or turn-down collars. Reversible ones were also available from mail-order companies such as Sears & Roebuck (USA) who, in 1897, advertised 'reversible four-in-hands in pure China silk, alike on both sides and reversible…in very nobby patterns'.

In the early twentieth century British square-ended ties were made of knitted silk and were referred to as 'Derbys', as in a Welch Margetson advertisement for 'Reversible Derbys' in 1908. They were either self-coloured or with different coloured bars or cross stripes (plate

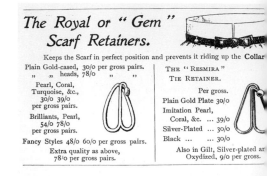

Rich Knitted Silk Cravats.

MACCLESFIELD MANUFACTURE.

52 opposite Royal or Gem
scarf retainers (1908);
Duplex tie frame (1916).
Details from Welch
Margetson catalogues of
1908 and 1916. T.80–1981;
T.85–1981

53 right Knitted silk cravats,
known as 'Derby's'. Colour
plate from the Welch
Margetson menswear
catalogue of 1910, p.103
T.81–1981

53). These knitted silk ties have retained their popularity because they make a good firm knot and keep their shape. There were also some woven silk ties which were almost square ended, with a cut-off sloping edge. These seem to have been unlined with broad blades and hemmed open ends. They appeared to be made from a scarf or square, but had shaped and stitched neckbands.

Tie Fashions of Europe and America 1890s -1940s

A wide range of ties was available to the American market judging by the Sears & Roebuck catalogue of 1897, although the range depended largely on the variety of fabrics rather than styles. The Teck scarf, already referred to as a ready-made tie using the sailor's knot, was made in two styles with broad and narrow blades, but nearly always with square ends (plate 54). Black silk ones sold for 50c each or 3 for $1.35 whilst coloured ones were 35c each or 3 for 1$. The firm also sold long ties, 1 inch (2.5cms) wide and 36 inches (91cms) long with square ends, that were known as 'Club House Ties' made from patterned China silk. Particular notice was given that they did *not* come in plain black or white. It was also claimed that these ties were suitable for women to wear with shirt-waists. These ties were offered at 14c each or six assorted patterns for 75c. American women also wore the broad bladed Windsor tie, which was 5 inches (13cms) wide and 36 inches (91cms) long. 'Windsor Ties are used by men, ladies and children, they are always popular for summer wear. Nothing is nicer for negligee shirts, ladies' waists or children's blouses.' This American Windsor Tie was not related to the later Windsor Knot.

By the 1920s, ties across Europe were displaying a rich and varied range of colours and patterns (plate 55). In France, such ties as the clip-on shown in plate 56 appeared, while the Isle von Scheel tie in plate 58 and the Picasso tie of plate 57 all show the diversity and flamboyance of fashionable ties at this time.

During the 1930s, however, colour and design became more restrained. The Depression in the USA of the late 1920s and early 1930s may have affected the quality and range of styles. Colours were more and more frequently restricted to the muted fashionable colours

54 below Teck ties, advertised in a Sears & Roebuck catalogue of 1897.

Black Teck Scarfs.

No. 2220. Men's Fine Black Silk or Satin Teck Scarfs, with flowing ends. Our own special importation, and we offer them at just one-half their regular retail value. All made up first-class and guaranteed to satisfy. Price, each...................25c

No. 2221. If you are in search of a rich jet black silk or heavy satin teck scarf, something that you usually pay a dollar to get but do not feel like paying it this season, order one of these scarfs at 50c and if you do not think it a bargain return it to us at our expense and we will cheerfully return you your money. These scarfs are made from extra heavy and fine black satin or silk, as desired, and heavily silk lined. They are elegantly made up in full teck shape, some with pointed and some with square ends. All are first quality in every way. Price, each...........50c; 3 for.............$1.35

Our 35c All Silk Tecks.

A SUPERB BLENDING OF PRICE AND QUALITY.

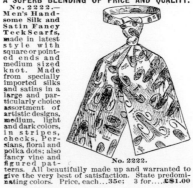

No. 2222.— Men's Handsome Silk and Satin Fancy Teck Scarfs, made in latest style with square or pointed ends and medium sized knot. Made from specially imported silks and satins in a large and particularly choice assortment of artistic designs, medium, light and dark colors, in stripes, checks, Persians, floral and polka dots; also fancy vine and figured patterns. All beautifully made up and warranted to give the very best of satisfaction. State predominating colors. Price, each...35c; 3 for....£$1.00

of the day – chiefly browns, golds, greens, blues and a dull red. Self-coloured ties rather than variegated colours appeared more often, whilst designs were usually restricted to checks and stripes or small repeating patterns. Woven wool ties made in subdued but attractive colours and patterns became increasingly popular in the 1930s (plate 59). They appeared early in the decade and were originally intended for sports and countrywear, but were soon adopted for town dress, which meant that they had become acceptable as fashionable accessories.

Washable Ties and The Windsor Knot

The washable tie re-appeared in the 1930s. *Esquire Magazine*, describing its attributes, said:

A few years earlier wash ties had not been taken seriously, but now, in 1936, they had been improved in both design and construction. Wash neckwear, both four-in-hands and bows, was available in a twin-ply design which gave added strength and wrinkle resistance. Spiral seams in the new wash neckwear also prevented ripping, produced resilience, and added to the life of the tie. Finally, hand bar tacking eliminated that old bane of a wash-tie wearer, loose stitching that unravelled after the tie was laundered.

The washable ties, according to *Esquire Magazine*, proved to be as popular as bow ties and the 'big-knot four-in-hand' that eventually became known as the Windsor knot. Rather complex, it was created to make a large knot in an attempt to copy the one preferred by the Duke of Windsor (1894-1972). This was based on the mistaken assumption that the Duke had created a larger knot by adding an extra twist when tying. This misunderstanding was revealed by the Duke in an interview with Lord Lichfield. Asked about the knot he was supposed to have pioneered, he admitted that he had invented nothing of the sort: 'It was simply that he preferred his ties cut a little wider and lined with thicker silk which gave the impression of a fatter knot. It was other people believing that he had found a new knot, who simulated the effect with a complex series of twists and folds'. The Duke tied his tie in the usual way, i.e. using the slip knot.

55 opposite Hand-painted silk tie. British, 1915. By Winifred Mara Gill for the Omega Workshop.
Circ.442–1962

56 below Clip-on tie. French, 1910–20s.
T.357–1992

57 right Brown and grey woven silk tie, designed by Pablo Picasso. French, 1930s. T.260–1967

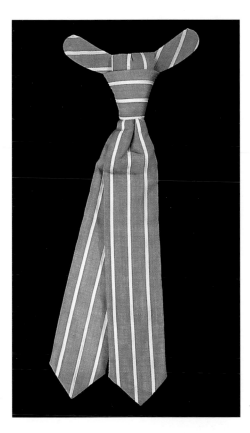

58 left Silk tie with batik
design by Ilse von Scheel.
German, 1920s. T.112–1969

59 opposite Rayon tie (left);
woven wool tie (right).
British, late 1930s / early
1940s. T.36–1982. T.270–1981

Chapter Six

Hand-painted, Square-ended and Couturier Ties, The Kipper, Artist-Designed Ties, Kitsch and Joke Ties 1940s – The Present Day

World War II and Utility Regulations

The Second World War (1939-45) brought about numerous restrictions, which inevitably affected the quality of many products for home consumption. In Britain the introduction in 1942 of the 'Utility' trademark (plate 60), with its distinctive sign 'C41', was intended to maintain a standard of quality set by the Board of Trade. (In America the War Production Board imposed guidelines for clothing manufacture, also in 1942, but only rubber goods and shoes were actually rationed). One of the effects on ties was the increased use of rayon (plate 61), since silk had been commandeered for the production of parachutes both in Britain and America. Wool continued to be used as it produced 'wrinkle-free' ties.

The Irish firm Richard Atkinson, which normally made high-quality poplin ties, turned their production over to making tweed ties: 'These sold well in America at $2.50, until Mexican ties arrived to sell at $1 each and killed the market for Irish tweed ties'. The economics of war meant that the home market had to increase productivity and earn currency from overseas by means of exports to neutral countries. Richard Atkinson's business before the war was 55 per cent home market and 45 per cent export. As early as 1940-41 their exports had increased by 10 per cent to 55 per cent. Because of restrictions

60 opposite Printed cotton tie. British, 1940s. Made by Tootal. Worn here with 1940s Utility collar, shirt and suit. Private collection

61 left Rayon tie, woven in
graduated diagonal stripes
of maroon, black and white.
British, 1940s–50s.
By Bolders of Oxford Street.
T.245–1996

imposed by the war, the company had its ties made abroad, in Australia and South Africa. Even then the raw material, rayon, had to be sent by cargo ship from Ireland.

The British tie manufactures, Michelsons (established in 1937 by Hans Wallach), started by producing scarves, but during the war also brought out a cheap range of ties at 6 pence each. The firm soon moved into the quality trade and began to provide ties for Austin Reed and Hornes Bros. Wallach recalled in 1945:

our exports were worth £1,166 and by 1966 had reached £250,000. We started to do the top-end trade about 1952 and the Hardy Amies range in 1959...It was his first venture into menswear along with Radiac shirts. Our cheapest tie today [1966/67] retails at twelve shillings and sixpence. Our turnover exceeds a million pounds a year and we sell over a million ties. Half of these are in silk, although they represent three-quarters of the business.

Tie styles of the 1960s are shown later in this chapter.

Hand-painted Ties

The hand-painted tie also became an accepted form of decoration in America during the war years. It enabled a man to express his own, sometimes deplorable, lack of taste (plate 62). *Esquire Magazine* described the type of hand-painted tie that appeared during the 1940s: 'It was seen in all sorts of patterns, everything from flowers to sailboats, and cost about $25. Such "art" demanded a larger-than-usual canvas, and most of these ties measured 4½ inches (11cms) in width, earning them the nicknames of "belly-warmer" and "scrambled egg" ties'. This wartime phenomenon continued to be popular for a few years after the war, and helped pave the way for the 'bold look' neckwear introduced in the fall of 1948. The *Saturday Evening Post* predicted in 1946 that wild ties would last at least another five years, since tie fashions went in cycles of seven to ten years. The wild designs of the 1940s were thought by psychologists to be a reflection of current world unrest.

In Europe the wide, boldly decorated tie became associated with the unsavoury Wide Boys or Spivs, men who operated in the black-market of the post-war period. Their loud ties, wide-shouldered, boldly striped baggy suits, two-tone shoes, pencil-thin moustaches and greased hair were really a development of the American zoot suit look of the late 1930s and 1940s. Nik Cohn described the English fashion as the 'American Look, based in the Charing Cross Road, sold

62 left 'Yacht' tie, printed rayon, 1940s. 'Hawaian Girl' tie, stencilled design on rayon, *c.*1951.
T.278–1992; T.208–1992

to a largely working class public'. This brash look was attractive to the young and the demobbed men after the war: it was a welcome release from the drabness of Utility and service uniforms.

In America enormous quantities of flamboyant ties were sold. The statistics are impressive. According to the Men's Tie Foundation and Men's Neckwear Manufacturers Association of America, there were over 600 manufacturers making ties in 1946, 200 million ties were sold in 1950 and there were 40,000 different patterns and 100,000 different colour ways.

The Edwardian Look, the Teddy Boy and the Wide Boy

In complete contrast to the Wide Boy look was the tailored Edwardian Look of the late 1940s and early 1950s. This was based on the regulation civilian dress of officers from British artillery regiments, whose dress consisted of a curly brimmed bowler hat, dark tailored suit, silk tie, the 'British warm' overcoat and a rolled umbrella. It was the Edwardian Look which inspired the British Teddy Boy fashions of the 1950s, a style popular with the younger generation. The ties which they wore were, as a rule, either narrow square-ended styles, or string or bootlace ties.

The square-ended tie was not worn solely by Teddy Boys: as a style it had survived from the 1930s and was still considered suitable for daywear with a suit or a sports jacket. By the late 1940s and early 1950s square-ended ties appeared in coloured silks woven in a variety of coloured stripes and checks. The most attractive styles came from Italy and France.

The English Edwardian style, with its shapely tailored cut, was an indication that the wide-shouldered loosely cut suit was on the way out. The accepted guideline to the width of a tie, according to Hans Wallach of Michelsons, is that it 'always corresponds with the width of the lapel'. In America the new fashion, which became known as the 'Mr T look', emphasised narrow shoulders, narrow tapered trousers and narrow ties with a small knot. This cut was developed further by European tailors and designers, creating a continental style of very short straight jackets (sometimes known as bum freezers), and even narrower tapered trousers. Short hairstyles and narrow-brimmed hats completed the overall appearance. As for ties, according to *Esquire Magazine* in 1952, they 'had slimmed down to 3½ inches [9cms] in width'. But by the end of the decade, it was quite usual for the square-ended styles to be as slim as 2 inches (5cms). This restraint had also affected tie patterns in the USA and Europe, and *Men's Wear* for autumn 1952 noted 'the trend in ties…as tending to sparsely patterned grounds in rather neat effects'. One of the more significant introductions was considered to be the new Dacron knits, which were sold as 'washable, nonwrinkle and no-stretch'.

Couturier Designs for Ties, 1950s Onwards

Times were changing, as is evident from a quick résumé by *Esquire Magazine* of tie designs from Europe in March 1959, in which they reported with some surprise: 'they are doing amazingly original things and yet at the same time these unconventional flights of fashion land by some creative miracle within the bounds of good taste'. Parisian designs included some lively prints inspired by famous works of art, well-known landmarks, and even grapes, wine bottles and wine glasses. Ties from Italy were predominantly black and gold, complimenting their fashionable black and gold shantung suits. English neckwear often had light grounds with dark stripes, and manufacturers were promoting mixtures of 'silky fleece and angora mohair…as noncrush, no-wrinkle ties' (plate 63).

The lively European designs reported by *Esquire Magazine*, with their varied and attractive colour schemes, were precursors of the changes to come in the 1960s. An important innovation was the growing interest shown by couturiers in designing and producing items of menswear. Christian Dior (1905–57) designed some distinctive neckties. Jacques Fath (1912–54) used his dress fabrics in imaginative ways: for instance, in the early 1950s, he took a claret coloured dress silk with black spots and overlayed it with black silk gauze to make a square-ended tie. He also designed colourful banded Indian silk ties.

In London, as early as 1957, Hardy Amies initiated a range of

63 opposite Four 1950s silk couturier ties. Left to right: woven red medallion on black, British, Hardy Amies; woven streaked pale blue and rust on black, French, Christian Dior; woven black and gold checks, British, Turnbull & Asser; woven ripple in shades of gold on black, French, Christian Dior. T.386:1–1992; T.374:1–1992; T.370–1992; T.371–1992

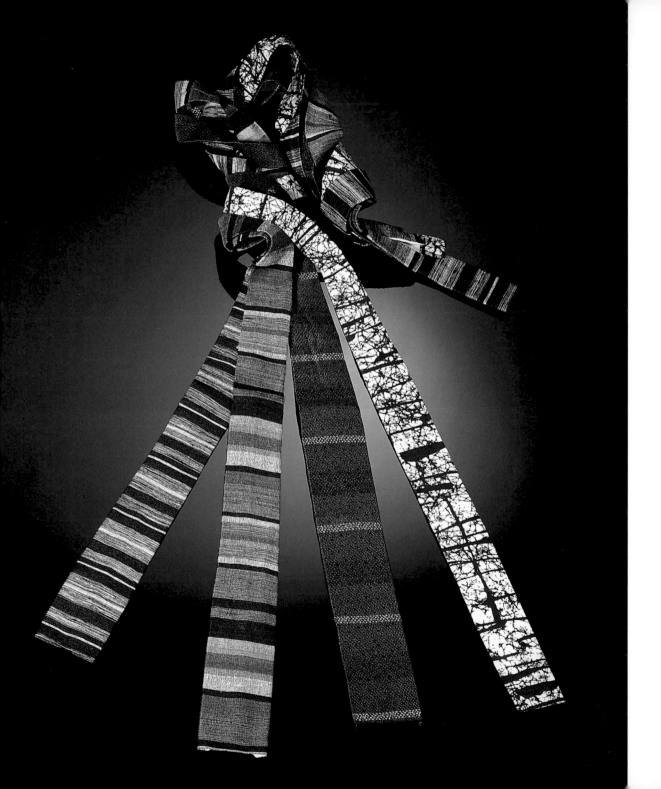

menswear designs for shirts and ties that appeared to those who wished to wear something original in contrast to the conservative greys of the 1950s. In 1960 he was invited to become design consultant to Hepworths, a multiple tailors with over 300 retail outlets in Britain, which later expaPnded to an international market, notable in the USA. Hardy Amies said:

Men all over the world want roughly the same thing, there are always slight variations...We cater for various publics. Hardy Amies ties sell for between forty-five shillings and three guineas. This is a different market to the Hepworth public. In America everything is geared to one group of people, below the luxury market but a cut above the High Street trade – the middle executive.

Always ahead of his time, Pierre Cardin opened his first men's boutique in 1957, and in 1960 he held his first men's collection of ready-to-wear-designer clothes. Included in this show were wide floral ties worn with 'lean look' suits. Cardin was one of the foremost designers to experiment with different types of fabric and with designs not usually considered suitable for ties. He broke the mould with a tan coloured silk tie woven in a lace pattern, produced between 1957 and 1960. Another of his ties was of printed cotton, with an abstract design of speckled squares overprinted in shades of purple, produced about 1959-60. Cardin was to revive these narrow square-ended ties some twenty years later, when he wore 'his own silky knit version. He was to be followed then as he was in the late 1950s and early '60s. As ties became wider in the late 1960s, square-ended ties followed suit.

The concept of wide floral ties introduced by Cardin in *c.*1960 did not catch on until the late 1960s and the inspiration of the kipper ties by Michael Fish. The jaunty equivalent for the 1950s and early 1960s were the much narrower square-ended ties, made in a surprising variety of fabrics with equally varied patterns. They ranged from fashionable printed cottons to rich silk dress silks and even leather.

The 1960s kipper ties tended to eclipse the square-ended ties, although floral printed cotton and silk examples were produced. The tradition of square-ended knitted silk or wool ties re-appeared in fashionable widths reaching 3–4 inches (8–10cms).

64 opposite Group of square-ended ties. Left to right: black and white bars in Indian silk, British 1965, Woollands; multicoloured bars in Indian silk, British 1960, Frank Johnson; green and blue silk with gilt metal thread, Italian 1950s, Vismara; blue-black wax batik in cotton, American 1963, Ernst.
T.681–1996; T.380–1992; T.260–1996; T.680–1996

65 left Group of 1960s
painted silk ties. Left to right:
Liberty, British, *c.*1960;
Liberty, British, early 1960s;
Harry Napper for Liberty,
British, 1966; John Michael,
British, 1966–70; 'Hung-on-
You', French, late 1960s;
Mr Fish, British, 1966–7;
Hayward, British, 1967–8.

T.198–1979; T.183–1979;

T.199–1979; T.202–1979;

T.314–1979; T.706–1979;

T.365–1979

The 1960s, Michael Fish and Kipper Ties

The unforgettable, wild kipper ties were worn between 1966 and 1973 (plate 66). The first was designed by Michael Fish when he worked at Turnbull & Asser. The term 'kipper' was a pun on his name. He stated, 'Very few people have had ties in their hearts like I've had…Ties were part of my uniform…Shape, length, width and colour were very important'. In 1966 he opened his own shop in Clifford Street, where he sold suits and ties of his own design. Sadly, this venture lasted only three years, but the shop was a great success: his turnover during that period eventually reached over £250,000 a year.

The 1960s, the Influence of Pop Art and Pop Music

Tie designs were just one aspect of fashion that formed part of the youth cult that had its origins in the 1950s but blossomed in the 1960s. The designs were inspired by contemporary art such as Pop Art and Op Art, and by the pop music of groups such as The Beatles, and The Rolling Stones. Some men chose to wear a combination of shirt and tie that created the Op Art effect (plate 67). Other influences were of social and political origin, like the hippie movement, combined with the increased use of recreational drugs. Hippies and drugs were linked with the anti-war movement that originated in the USA in the late 1960s as a reaction to America's involvement in the Vietnam War between 1964 and 1975. Some of the psychedelic designs and colours that typify the late 1960s were originally inspired by drugs. Other sources of inspiration were derived from the Art Nouveau style of the late nineteenth and early twentieth century. Most couturiers recognised the commercial possibilities and found a useful outlet in the popular demand for colourful neckwear. Emilio Pucci in particular produced wonderful ties from his fabrics. His highly individual designs transposed successfully into a seemingly endless supply of exotic ties (plate 68). The group by John Stephen in plate 69 provide a good example of the change from the vibrant colours of the 1960s to the more sombre '70s but maintaining the kipper width and strong bold designs. A favourite outfit at this time of Sir Roy Strong (former director of the V&A) is shown in plate 70.

66 above Kipper tie.
British, 1966–7. Mr Fish.
T.706–1974

67 opposite Silk check tie,
French, late 1960s,
Yves St Laurent; striped
shirt, British, late 1960s,
Turnbull & Asser.
T.353–1979. T.368–1979

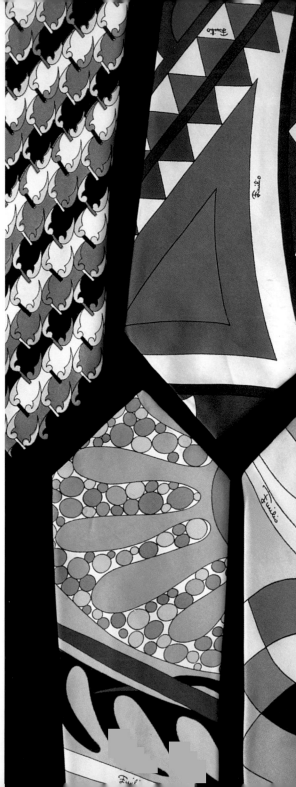

68 right Group of silk ties.
Italian, late 1960s.
By Emilio Pucci. T.453–1985;
T.454–1985; T.455–1985;
T.456–1985; T.457–1985;
T.458–1985; T.459–1985;
T.460–1985; T.461–1985;
T.462–1985

69 opposite Printed silk and
cotton kipper ties.
British, early 1970s.
By John Stephen. T.226–1997.
T.224–1997. T.225–1997

70 right Brown silk tie,
British, *c.*1972, Turnbull &
Asser; shirt *c.*1970; suit
1968. This ensemble was
worn in the early 1970s
by Sir Roy Strong.
Tie: T.207–1979

The 1970s and 1980s: The Tie Report and Tie Rack

As the exuberance of the styles of the late 1960s and early 1970s gradually gave way to more restrained and formal designs, ties became narrower, returning to 2–3 inches (5–7.5cms) in width, with subdued decoration. Alan Flusser stipulates that the

proper width of a tie, and one that will never be out of style, is 3 1/4 inches [8cms] (2 3/4 to 3 1/2 inches [7–9cms] are also acceptable)…Though many of the neckties sold today are cut in these widths, the section of the tie where the knot is made has remained thick – a holdover from the fat, napkin like ties of the 1960s.

Traditional designs of the 1930s and 1950s reappeared, such as small geometric motifs and paisley patterns.

New ideas revolved around ties designed for a shirt and sold together as a colour co-ordinated package. Decoration was minimal and restricted to the area just below the knot. Attractive colour combinations began to appear, such as the early 1980s knitted ties by Ermenegildo Zegna, who produced a square-ended tie of knitted beige cotton with diagonal stripes in red, orange and blue, and another by Prochownick of pink cotton with cream and beige banded decoration (plate 72). With brilliant, usually printed, patterns, ties were also gradually increasing in width in proportion to wider jacket lapels. The tie printed with a detail from a painting by Boucher, shown in plate 71, shows how Vivienne Westwood interpreted this trend.

However, this preference for brighter and wider ties does not seem to have been evinced by the average Englishman or his family. In 1989 the *Portsmouth News* reported that in Britain the average man preferred blue ties, either plain or perhaps paisley or striped, and went on to query, 'Where does that leave those trying to reintroduce the 1960s Paisley kipper monstrosities?' Another local newspaper, the *Derby Evening Telegraph*, asked various men about their taste in ties in October 1989, one of whom admitted 'I'm a real tie-aholic, My daughters have relegated all my kipper ties but I've hidden them at the bottom of my wardrobe'.

These comments are taken from the Tie Report, compiled by Tie

71 opposite Printed silk tie, with design taken from the painting *Venus and Adonis* by François Boucher (1736–82). British, 1991. By Vivienne Westwood. T.24–1991

72 left Square-ended
knitted ties. Early 1980s.
By Ermenegildo Zegna and
Prochownick.
T.228–1986; T.229–1986

73 opposite Printed silk tie
with design of Fame with
putti and garlands. British,
1994. By Paul Smith.
T.188–1995

Rack in 1989. As well as surveying British men's taste in ties, the report also compared their tie-buying habits with that of American men. Tie Rack was founded in Britain in 1981 by Roy Bishko as tie and scarf retailers, and had expanded its franchises to the USA in 1987. By 1989 forty shops had opened across the States. The report claims that 'American men own, on average, 22 ties, compared with the British average of 17'. The report also revealed that the British obsession with class structure was never far away: 83 per cent of British men claimed to be able to tell a man's social standing from his tie, whilst only 45 per cent of Americans made the same claim.

When the designer Paul Smith (plate 73) opened one of his menswear shops in Covent Garden, London, in 1987, Judy Rumbold for the *Guardian* newspaper reported that, 'he talks with awesome enthusiasm of his passion for ties. An absolutely massive "tie selection will be accommodated…every spot, stripe and combination of the two will be exploited, and the mills in Como where most of the tie fabrics are woven, are a source of great excitement"'. His enthusiasm was justified, as in 1987 he recorded the 'average weekly sale in one shop alone of 120 ties'. He attributed this figure to the fact that more men were wearing suits than before. Fashion had changed again – Judy Rumbold, writing again in 1987, explained the earlier decline of tie wearing thus: 'Ties lost popularity in 1972 when men would go to work in open-necked shirts that had high rounded collars. The advent of the roll neck sweater also made ties redundant'.

The discriminating man who prefers original ties and is not afraid of bold designs is more likely to appreciate ties that are designed by artists and can be made to order. The tie designed by Picasso (plate 57) has a brown silk ground with the design woven in silvery grey. The same design was also produced in blue and grey. Another designer tie, also in the V&A, is the silk batik from about 1921 designed by Ilse von Scheel, who worked with Van der Velde (plate 58). Salvador Dali produced surrealist designs in the 1940s for the American tie manufacturer James Lehrer.

In Britain, Europe and the USA in the 1980s and 1990s a taste developed for increasingly unusual tie designs. These ranged from the

74 opposite Hand-painted silk ties. British, from left to right: 1987, 1990, 1989. By Vicky Holton. T.41–1992. T.42–1992. T.43–1992

deliberate kitsch to those designed and produced by artists. Amongst contemporary British designers are Hugh Dunford Wood and Vicky Holton, who both produce their own ties and design to order. Their work is original and distinctive: Hugh Dunford Wood uses acid dyes in brilliant colours, whilst Vicky Holton works with extruded paint using an impasto technique and spirit-based paint (plate 74).

Manufacturers have also had fun producing kitsch designs which have become increasingly bizarre. An American company produced a transparent, plastic ready-made tie that represented gambling: sealed inside the tie were gambling chips, playing cards and dice (plate 75). Indonesia produces exotic, ready-made feather ties, probably aimed at the tourist trade (plate 76). Examples that reach Europe appear to have been brought back as presents, and are worn only as a joke, not as fashion.

As for choosing a tie, it seems that most men, whether in the UK or the USA, prefer to select their own, on their own. Alan Flusser dedicated his book, *Clothes and the Man*, 'To the women in my life: Marilese, Janet, Rita, Skye and Peper, all of whom I love dearly, none of whom I'd send to buy me a tie'.

British Tie Production

Tie production in the UK between 1986 and 1989 ranged between 21,513,000 pieces in 1986 and 24,456,000 in 1989; 1988 proved to be the best year when 25,389,000 ties were produced. However, 9,409,000 pieces were imported in 1988 compared with 4,293,000 exported.

British tie manufacturer Paul John, unlike companies such as Atkinsons (Belfast) or Michelsons (London), is quite a young firm, and began as, and still is, a family concern. Founded in the late 1960s, by 1991 it had grown into a company that employed 25 people and produced 2000 ties a day. They continually design and invest in their own technology to streamline the production. They design their own ties and also act as distributors for other designers such as Roberto Moschino (plate 77), Punch and Katharine Hamnett. Their own ties are sold nationwide to large stores, including Liberty's, Harrods and Harvey Nichols, as well as to boutiques.

75 opposite, left 'Gambler's tie' of clear plastic, with sealed-in playing cards, chips and dice. American, 1987–9. By Tie Guys. T.211–1992

76 opposite, right Ready-made tie of various feathers. Indonesian, 1980s. By Gun Yeu. T.212–1992

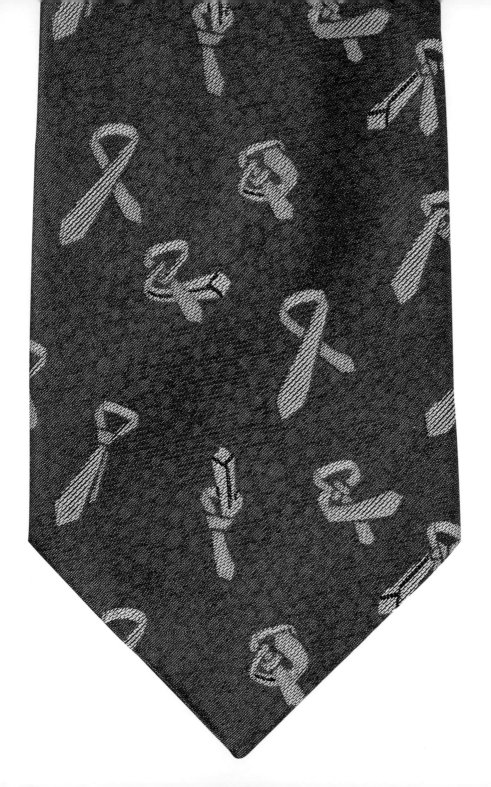

77 left Silk tie with woven design of four-in-hand knot. Italian, 1991. By Roberto Moschino. T.141–1991

Postscript

Tying the Knot

Tying a tie, whether it is the cravat, the long tie or the bow tie, has always presented problems. All tie books and articles since *Neckclothitania* in 1818 show how to tie the different knots, making use of descriptions with pictures or diagrams. (Plate 77 provides an amusing comment on this phenomenon.) Connoisseurs of dress have offered advice and even laid down rules for the correct appearance of the knot. These authors have been concerned that a well-tied tie should distinguish the wearer and set him apart from other men. The author of *Neckclothitania* wrote in his preface: 'I have been induced to publish the following observations on the nature of Ties from a sincere and earnest wish of seeing a distinct line drawn between *l'homme comme il faut*, and *la canaille*'. Alan Flusser prefers the slip knot above all other knots: 'It is the smallest and most precise of knots…it has been the staple of British-American style of dress…for the past fifty years', and 'should be tied so that there is a dimple or crease in the centre of the tie just below the knot. This forces the tie to billow and creates a fullness that is the secret to its proper draping.'

The interest in the tie lies not only in the knots and the design - it is more than sartorial, since the tie also serves as a label, offering an insight on the man himself. An item of dress so close to the face cannot avoid notice, and therefore either by its presence or absence a man is automatically assessed. His taste or lack of it is under judgement, even his politics, education or sporting achievements can be deduced. As long as the tie and the suit are worn, a man's character and taste will continue to be judged by his choice of tie and the quality of the knot. Lawrence Langner, author of *The Importance of Wearing Clothes*,

summing up the importance of the tie, wrote 'The answer is that the necktie is a symbol of a man's superiority, for be sure that in selecting and wearing a tie, he reveals his conservatism or bohemianism, or some other attitude towards life, and even in his day-by-day selection of the tie to wear, he fits the apparel to his mood'. It is not hard to imagine the mood required to wear the tie in plate 78!

While the future of the long tie is being questioned by the man in the street, manufacturers and designers are keen that it should continue. They encourage its existence by creating designs that are attractive and desirable. Professional groups and older men who are used to traditional styles of dress expect to wear a tie. Younger generations are less inhibited and many do not have or need to wear one. The yuppie of the late 1980s created a market for designer ties within the normally conservative taste of the city environment, a fashion that survived into the 1990s (plate 79). Menswear departments of shops have a wide range of designer ties, while exclusive shops or boutiques are noted for their unusual ties commissioned especially for their label.

Ties, when worn, still have a certain cachet for the wearer, for the choice of tie still indicates the type of person. Colour and design are most important; quality is very telling (plate 80). A well-designed and expensive tie commands notice, indicating a man of taste who cares about his appearance and appreciates quality. After three hundred years of wearing neckties, the importance of neckwear and the consciousness of its impact on the observer has hardly changed. George Etherege in his play of 1676, *The Man of Mode*, required his fashion-conscious anti-hero, Dorimant, to declare: 'That a man's excellency should lie in neatly tying of a ribbon or a cravat! How careful's nature in furnishing the world with necessary coxcombs'.

78 opposite Printed pink satin rayon tie. British, 1950s. T.502–1992

79 below Tie of woven bee design. British, 1992. By Michelson. T.418–1992

80 left Pair of printed silk ties. Left: 'Patch'; right; 'Red Horses'. British, 1990–91. By Caroline Charles.

T.12–1991; T.10–1991

Glossary

*Where terms have been italicised
they have an entry of their own*

Ascot Square-ended tie, with each end of equal width. It consists of two knots: the first is a single knot, the second is formed by making a loop at the top of one end through which the other end is passed, creating a barrel shaped knot. The knot is then adjusted by pulling both ends downwards, crossing them over each other and fastening with a pin. Ready-made Ascots are stylised versions of this knot.

Bag-wig Black silk bag with a draw-string, used to enclose the plait or 'queue' of hair. A stiff bow at the nape of the neck concealed the draw-string. The bag protected clothing from any gease or powder on the wig.

Band Seventeenth-century term, originally for plain *linen* collars that required a support about the neck. It could also refer to the upright band of the shirt collar. The term was also applied in the late seventeenth century to the bibbed band of lace or plain linen.

Band strings Fine decorative cords used to tie the *band* or *cravat* at the neck. Often finished with elaborate tassels, and usually bought in pairs. Could also be of ribbon when tying a cravat.

Bandanna Coloured or patterned *neckcloth*, from the nineteenth century, originally made in India using the tie-dye (or wax-resist) method of dying. Early examples were of silk but later European ones were often of printed *cotton*.

Belcher Neckcloth named after the boxer James Belcher (1791-1811),

who made Indian silk neckcloths fashionable.

Blade Term used in the tie trade to describe the pointed ends of the *long tie*. An alternative term is *tab*.

Bone lace English term used to identify *bobbin lace*. Bobbins were often made of bone.

Bobbin lace Type of lace made by plaiting and twisting together threads wound onto small bobbins attached to a firm pillow. Another term for this is *pillow* or *bone lace*.

Cambric see *linen*.

Canvas see *linen*.

Chitterlings Nineteenth century slang term for shirt frills.

Cloak band Very broad *linen* collar fashionable in the 1630s. Draped over the upright doublet collar and reaching the shoulders, it looked not unlike the cape of a cloak.

Cotton Term applied to various fabrics all made from a spun fibre taken from the sub-tropical cotton plant. First developed in India. The quality of the yarn or thread varies; the finest is produced in Egypt and Sea Island, Georgia USA. The spinning and weaving determines the quality of the fabric which can be as fine as *muslin* or as coarse as *canvas*.

Cravat Late seventeenth-century term (?French) in use from 1650s onwards. The Oxford English Dictionary describes it as a derivation from 'Croat' adopted for the neckwear worn in imitation of Croatian mercenaries. Describes a long *neckcloth* that is either tied in a bow at the neck or tied by a bow of a separate ribbon or *band string*. The term 'cravatte' has continued

to be used in France when referring to any fashionable neckwear.

Dowlas see linen.

Faille French term applied to a soft corded silk.

Falling band Plain or finely pleated *linen* collar, that is turned down over the doublet collar and does not require any support.

Four-in-hand One of several names for the *slip knot*, used to knot the *long tie* at the end of the nineteenth century and the early twentieth century. The term was used in Britain and is still used in the USA.

Fuller's Earth 'it is of great use in scouring cloths, stuffs etc. lmblbing all the grease and oil' (Dictionary of Arts and Sciences, 1754, vol. II, part II, p.1352).

Holland see *linen*

Jabot Frills worn down the front of the shirt, made of lace or of *lawn*. Eighteenth century.

Lawn see *linen*

Linen Yarn made from the fibres of the flax plant. The plant is allowed to rot in water to separate the fibres, which are then spun into yarn or thread. As both a fibre and a textile, linen has been known throughout history. The fabrics made of linen are known as *linen, lawn, cambric, holland, canvas and dowlas*. The finest linens, used for neckwear, were linen, lawn and cambric; cambric was the finest quality and the most expensive.

Long tie Interlined tie that has been made from two or three pieces of fabric with open pointed ends. The fabric is cut on the cross, joined together, and folded and pressed flat.

Muscadin Name given to a group of fops or dandies in France at the time of the Revolution. Whether or not they were called 'Muscadin' after musk perfume is uncertain.

Muslin Finely woven *cotton* fabric.

Neckcloth Very long narrow cloth of fine *linen* or *muslin* with fringed, tasselled or lace finished ends. It was wrapped once about the neck and tied in a simple knot, with the ends either allowed to hang loose down the front of the chest or twisted and poked into the coat buttonhole like the *steinkirk*.

Needle lace Lace that is built up stitch by stitch on an outline structure of thick threads tacked along the lines of a design, drawn out on a parchment pattern.

Octagon Ready-made tie in the style of the *Ascot*, formed around a pasteboard *stiffener*. It had eight sides which rotated around a pin, allowing the wearer to use each of the eight sides or edges in turn.

Pillow lace Alternative term for *bone lace*.

Rep or **Repp** Term for a corded fabric of *silk*, silk and wool, or *cotton* mixture.

Sailor's knot Term for the *slip knot*, so named as it was one of the knots used by sailors to tie their *neckcloths*. It should not be confused with the reef knot. The name was adopted for the fashionable *long tie* at the end of the nineteenth century and continued to be used in the early twentieth century.

Scarf or shawl cravat Ready-made *cravat*, fashionable in the nineteenth century. Made with a stiffened upright collar and fastened by a buckle at the back of the neck. So named because of the exceptionally long pendant bibs, gathered onto the collar, that draped over the shirt front completely covering it.

Scarf ring Often a finger ring, used instead of a knot to fasten a scarf by passing the ends through it.

Shirt waist The blouse and skirt became fashionable dress in the 1890s. *Shirt waist* is a contemporary American term for the blouse, which sometimes fitted onto a waistband.

Silk Lustrous fibre produced from the cocoon of the caterpillar (bombyx mori) of bombycidae moths, which feed on mulberry leaves; the silk fibre is produced by the caterpillar (silk worm) when making a cocoon prior to the pupae stage. The Chinese were the first to discover the properties of the cocoon as early as 2600 BC. The technology of producing silk reached Europe in the Middle Ages but for centuries the raw materials had to be imported from the East.

Slip knot Knot most commonly used today, to tie the *long tie*. The tie is placed around the neck, leaving the left end longer than the right. The left end is passed over the right, and brought round to the front and passed over again so that the two ends are being bound together. The left end is passed over again, bringing it through to the front above the beginning of the knot, pushed down under the uppermost layer and pulled through to form the knot. The knot can be adjusted by sliding it up and down on the right end whilst keeping it taught.

Solitaire Black ribbon tied in a bow at the front of the neck, over a *stock*. Worn as a rule with the *bag wig*, in the eighteenth century.

Steinkirk Long *neckcloth* with the ends twisted and poked into the coat buttonhole. Named after the battle of Steinkirk in 1692.

Stiffener Oblong form with rounded ends which was placed inside the *stock* (iii) at the front of the neck. It could be made of pasteboard, whalebone strips, leather, buckram or a quilted cotton pad.

Stock (i) Upright neckband of a shirt, from the seventeenth, eighteenth and nineteenth centuries.

(ii) Fashionable item of eighteenth-century neckwear, made from a rectangle of fine white pleated *linen* which was gathered on to flat linen *tabs* attached at each end, and fastened at the back of the neck with a *stock buckle*, a button or tapes.

(iii) Neckwear of the nineteenth century made of black, white or coloured silk or fine *linen*, usually tied with a bow at the front and with a stiffened interlining. Could be hand-tied or ready-made. Ready-made examples were fastened by a buckle at the back of the neck.

Stock buckle Metal buckle used to fastened the *stock* (ii) at the back of the neck.

Tab Term used to describe the pointed ends of the *long tie*. An alternative term is *blade*.

Waterfall cravat Hunting *cravat*, tied once about the neck in a half knot, and puffed out under the chin. Fastened with a cravat pin.

Major UK Dress Collections that include Neckwear

Gallery of English Costume,
Platt Hall,
Rusholme,
Manchester

Museum of Costume,
Assembly Rooms,
Bath

Museum of Costume and Textiles,
Castle Gate,
Nottingham

Museum of London,
London Wall,
London

Victoria and Albert Museum,
South Kensington,
London

Welsh Folk Museum,
St Fagan's,
Cardiff

There are many other museums which collect historic and contemporary dress but which do not have the space or facilities for display. Enquiries can be made at your local museum or library. For UK collections you may be able to obtain a copy of Janet Arnold's guide to the study of dress and to relevant collections, *A Handbook of Costume* (London, Macmillan 1973; New York, S.G. Phillips 1980). Both UK and US editions are now sadly out of print, however.

Selected Bibliography

A Cavalry Officer *The Whole Art of Dress...* (London 1830)

Anon. *Necklothitania ; or; tittania: being an essay on starchers; by one of the cloth* (London, J.J. Stockdale 1818)

Anon. *Dress and Address* (London, J.J. Stockdale 1819)

Barney, Sydney *Clothes and the Man: a guide to correct dress for all occasions* (London, Sir Isaac Pitman 1951).

Bennet-England, Rodney *Dress Optional: the revolution in menswear* (London, Peter Owen 1967).

Blanc, H. le *The Art of Tying the Cravat* (London, Effingham Wilson & Ingrey & Madeley 1828; Bonn, Thullverlag 1989)

Chaille, François *The Book of Ties* (Paris, Flammarion, reprinted 1997)

Clarke, Philip *Ties are their business* (Belfast, Richard Atkinson & Co. Ltd 1970)

Cole, Hubert *Beau Brummell* (London, Granada Publishing 1977)

Cunnington, C.W. and P. *Handbook of English Costume in the 17th Century* (London, Faber & Faber, reprinted 1972)

Cunnington, C.W. and P. *Handbook of English Costume in the 18th Century* (London, Faber & Faber, reprinted 1972)

Cunnington, C.W. and P. *Handbook of English Costume in the 19th Century* (London, Faber & Faber, reprinted 1970)

Cunnington, C.W. and P. *The History of Underclothes* (London, Michael Joseph 1951)

Curtis. G.F. *Clothes and the Man* (London, Jonathan Cape, reprinted 1940)

Dyer, Rod and Spark, Ron *Fit to be Tied: vintage ties of the forties and early fifties* (New York, Abbeyville Press 1987)

Flusser, Alan *Clothes and the Man* (New York, Villard Books 1988)

Gale, W. and Schoeffler, O.E. (eds) *Esquire's Encyclopedia of 20th-century Men's Fashions* (McGraw Hill 1973)

Gibbings, Sarah *The Tie* (Studio Editions 1990)

Jesse, Captain *The Life of Beau Brummel* (London, The Navarre Society Ltd 1927, 2 volumes)

Latham, R. and Matthew, W. (eds) *The Diary of Samuel Pepys* (London, Bell & Co Ltd 1970, 1971, 1973, 1983)

Laver, James *Schools, University, Navy, Army, Air-Force and Club Ties* (London, Seeley Service & Co Ltd 1968)

Levey, Santina *Lace: A History* (W.S. Maney & Son Ltd and the Victoria & Albert Museum 1983)

Levitt, Sarah *Victorians Unbuttoned: registered designs for clothing, their makers and wearers, 1839-1900* (London, Allan and Unwin, reprinted 1986)

Moers, Ellen *The Dandy: Brummell to Behrbohm* (London, Secker & Warberg 1960)

Mosconi, Davide and Villarosa, Riccardo *The Book of Ties: 188 knots for necks; history, techniques* (London, Tie Rack 1985)

Pellegrin, Nicole *Les Vêtements De La Liberte 1780-1800* (Aix-en-Provence, Alinea 1989)

Punch, or The London Charivari (London, magazine founded in 1841)

Stop, Monsieur et Madame *Manuel Complet de la Toilette: ou l'art de s'habiller avec élégance et méthode, contenant l'art de mettre sa cravate, e.t.c.* (Paris 1828)

The Tailor and Cutter (London, magazine founded in 1866)

Index

Illustrations are indicated by page numbers in italics